"I love what Lonnie ha[s been] able to take people fro[m ...] [...and bring them to] life with a whole new perspective. She uses what is admittedly fictional back stories, but as I read them I began to see real people with real needs encountering a loving Jesus. I think this book is a great way to encourage us to take these encounters from scripture and make them more personal - to bring them to life. I simply love this book."

PHILLIP WARD
Senior Pastor
Worship Leader
The River Church at Jacksonville
www.Riverjax.com
Worship CDs: *The Rebekah Project; Open the Door;* and *Rivers in the Desert*

"In the book, Jesus – Life Changer! Lonnie gives a wonderful imaginary background to the New Testament characters which she has so creatively woven into a Hebraic context. The characters of the stories become more personal and the reality much closer. The stories reflect the compassion of Adonai and as I read them my heart was deeply touched."

ALYOSHA RYABINOV
International Concert Pianist and Speaker
Author: *Thinking Hebraically.*
CDs: *Abba; Eli Eli; Upon the Bells of the Horses*; and more.
Available on:
www.SongofIsrael.com

"What a joy and delight to read these stories of Biblical characters through Lonnie Lane's eyes of revelation from Yeshua! As I turned each page, I kept hearing this truth: We live, we have questions, we search for truth and love, and Yeshua ENCOUNTERS us, and our lives are gloriously changed forever!! Yeshua IS truth, and His truth does bring LIFE! Lonnie also beautifully weaves in life from a Jewish perspective. She is a prophetic writer, and revelation bursts forth from these stories. Oh, the Power and Glory of Yeshua's Love! - it transcends everything! Love wins hearts and does change lives! Lonnie writes with wisdom, insight, and understanding of Yeshua. It is my honor to call her friend, and especially, my Aglow sister in the One, True Living God!"

DEBORAH SMITH
President of NE Area Team
Aglow International.
deborahsmithaglow@gmail.com

"JESUS - LIFE CHANGER! brings to life the humanity of characters close to Jesus while He walked the earth. Journeying inside their thoughts and motives Lonnie addresses the very struggles and victories they could have felt while encountering the Man Jesus. Her stories cause the imagination to soar and allows our hearts to experience Emmanuel (Adonai with us) through the eyes of those He loved."

MARK PULLEN
Jacksonville House of Prayer
www.jaxhop.com

"I have a note written in my Bible at the phrase in Matthew 4:13, 'Then Jesus arrived from Galilee...' I wrote, 'and everything changed.' When I'm studying the Word, I enjoy being led by the Holy Spirit to meditate between the lines to experience what might have been. That's what Lonnie has done as she wrote JESUS - LIFE CHANGER! The characters in each of the stories are clearly seen in their 1st century Hebrew culture as she describes how their lives were radically changed by their brief but intimate contact with Jesus. Lonnie reveals their deepest personal thoughts by being led by the Holy Spirit 'between the lines.' Be prepared to have your heart touched by the Spirit as you read. I'm glad I resisted the urge to jump ahead to Part II. It was worth the wait."

JOHN MAGWOOD
Former YWAM Missionary
Billy Graham Evangelistic Association Rapid Response Team Counselor

"In this very creative work Lonnie takes us on a behind the scenes look at some of the most well-known Bible stories. This book is sure to give the reader an entirely new perspective on the Bible and empower the reader to see past tradition. After reading this you too will want to begin trying to consider the unmentioned back stories in the Biblical narrative. Thumbs Up!"

TAPANI M. KYMALAINEN
Co-host of: Bent Ear/YouTube.com.
Author of: The Genesis Mousetrap and The Empires of Image.

"Lonnie has taken her knowledge of the Bible, along with Adonai given inspirations, and written some of the most intriguing stories I have ever read. I would highly recommend this book to the newest believer, and especially to those long-term believers. Who of us hasn't ever wondered what life might have been like, when Jesus was on the earth? Her insights into the stories she has written had me picking up my Bible. I envisioned myself on the streets of Jerusalem. Each character she portrayed has become very real to me."

B.J. BROOKS ROBINSON
Author of: *Audrey's Window; There's an Angel in the House; Unequally Yoked to AA (An Alcoholic);* and, *Adam's Choices* - sequel to *There's an Angel in the House*)

"Lonnie Lane has written a timeless saga which dives deeply into the minds and hearts of the early followers of Yeshua (Jesus). With compassion, curiosity and willingness to be vulnerable, she entertains and inspires us with the human, frail side of those early followers. The details of their lies, so eloquently expressed, display the timelessness of their stories. Lonnie brings readers to considering the invitation for growth and learning inherent in each story. The book is inspiring and showcases human nature in a marvelous way."

MINDY TATZ CHERNOFF
Founder of: The Resonant Horse–Healing & Leadership Development through Horses
Author of: From Muck to Magnificence
TedTalk Speaker
www.theresonanthorse.com

"At what part of your personal story do you wish Yeshua would have showed up? The stories told in the Bible focus on their teaching points. We don't always know what thoughts and feelings preceded them. Lonnie had captured that here, with some of the most famous stories in the Bible. She brings us into the possible scene that might have taken place behind the recorded one, and thus encourages all of us to invite Yeshua to come into our personal scenes and change them forever."

ORNA GRINMAN
Founder and Leader of Ot OoMofet (A Sign and an Example) Ministries
Author of: Hidden Faces of God; Woven With Gold; and Who is Knocking at Your Door?
www.ornagrinman.com

"This book offers a wider look at plausible conversations which likely may have taken place in the broader context of these well-known biblical accounts. An enjoyable, easy read for those who would like to let their imaginations wander along with the author into a more authentic cultural setting which makes the story all the more understandable and life-giving for its day.

COOKIE ISSAN
Executive Director
Makor HaTikvah Messianic School, Jerusalem
www.makorhatikvah.org

"Lonnie, you write with a sense of authority and profound inspiration. You are truly gifted both as a story teller and as a writer. Your opening narrative brought to mind "Fiddler on The Roof" relating the history of his village. Your writing is more than just inspired, it's as if you have been handed a script in which to narrate to your audience. It is obvious to me it is your belief that the script was indeed authored by Yeshua and you are merely the conduit thru which it travels. I enjoyed your very inspired writing although I am not a believer. There was a sense of authenticity in it."

HOWARD LADERMAN
Friend

"Lonnie Lane has taken a few of our favorite Bible stories and turned them into personal testimonies of the people involved, and she's done it in such a way that each one imparts hope to her readers for another powerful personal encounter with Jesus in their own lives. Thank you, Lonnie, for sharing your wonderful insights of human nature and weaving them like scarlet and gold threads throughout the fabric of our understanding of the Lord."

VICKI WHITE SMITH
Pastoral Counselor
www.freedomswayministries.com
Author of: The Counterfeit Kingdom: A False Principality with a Powerless king; Freedom is for Such a Time as Now: Discovering God's Plan for Restoration and Our Part in It, and Who's Using Your Tongue? - The Language of the Spirit World.

JESUS:
Life Changer!

Stories of Those
Who Knew Him

Biblical Fiction

LONNIE LANE

STOREHOUSE MEDIA GROUP, LLC

Jacksonville, Florida

JESUS: LIFE CHANGER! Stories of Those Who Knew Him

Copyright © 2018 by Lonnie Lane

All rights reserved by author. The author guarantees all content is original and do not infringe upon the legal rights of any other person or work. No part of this publication may be reproduced, distributed, or transmitted in any form or by any means, including photocopying, recording, or other electronic or mechanical methods, without the prior written permission of the Author, except in the case of brief quotations embodied in critical reviews and certain other noncommercial uses permitted by copyright law. For permission requests, email Author at email address below and type in subject line: "Attention: Permissions Coordinator."

Storehouse Media Group, LLC
Jacksonville, Florida
www.StorehouseMediaGroup.com
publish@StorehouseMediaGroup.com

Ordering Information:
Quantity sales. Special discounts are available with the Publisher at the email address above and type in subject line
"Special Sales Department."

Cover Design by Clara Anderson

The views expressed in this work are solely those of the author(s) and do not necessarily reflect the views of the publisher, and the publisher hereby disclaims any responsibility for them.

JESUS: LIFE CHANGER! Stories of Those Who Knew Him /
Lonnie Lane —1st ed.

ISBN: 978-1-943106-28-8 (paperback)
ISBN: 978-1-943106-29-5 (ebook)
Printed in the United States of America

To
Shirley & Bill

From
Janine

Many Blessings!

Date

Dedication

To the memory of my precious Mom

Nesbeth Lane

Also known as "Gra" (short for Gramom)

to those of us who loved her.

She enjoyed when I read her stories in the

last years of her life.

She would have loved these.

Acknowledgements

No one writes a book, or even lives their lives, out of their own inspiration or insight. We are all a composite of how we have been influenced by others along with way. Maybe we should all write an Acknowledgement page for those who have been a blessing to our own lives and send it to those on it. I get to do some of it here.

Most of all, to **Yeshua,** my Lord, My God, my everything – thank You for allowing me to be Yours. And for all the wonderful people You have put in my life.

My very special thanks to **Paul Wilbur** for your friendship and gracious words in the Foreword. It is an honor to be a part of your Prayer Support Team and to watch from there all that God has been unfolding prophetically. So much promise-fulfillment is yet ahead!

To **Pastor Phil Ward** who was willing to ordain me, and whose trust and support in many ways has enriched my life. Thank you, Phil, for opening the door for me to share in thirty-seven monthly Shabbat services, for all the Hebrew roots classes, the Passover Seders, and for the weekly prayer meetings for Israel and more. My thanks to you and **Pastor Evie** for your friendship. Thanks also for your insights into "Levi's" experience and your enthusiasm for the stories and that they could be used as one-act plays. What a great idea!

To **Pastor Sean Yost** for your warm welcome to me at Redeemer Church and your invitation to teach and much more. Most of all, I thank you for the faithful love you and **Barb** have continually extended to our family.

Thanks to **Melissa Gillespie** who so carefully went over the first draft, offering many comments and "fixes" to this book - and for your always-encouraging friendship.

My thanks to **Tapani Kymalainen, John Magwood, Alyosha Ryabinov, Mark Pullen, B.J. Robinson, Deborah Smith, Mindy Tatz Chernoff,** and **Vicki White Smith** who took the time to read through these stories and respond to them with your Reviews. Your accolades blessed me beyond my expectations. Appreciation also to **B.J., Mindy, and Vicki** whose editing insights helped to polish the book.

My additional appreciation goes as well to **Orna Grinman** for her insight and Israeli perspective. And to **Cookie Issan** for her editorial input, especially where my Hebrew was concerned. I thank you both for your kind Reviews as well.

Note: *I am often asked what ministries I would recommend donating to in Israel. Both those of Orna (to widows and* orphans) and Cookie (to the only Messianic school in Jerusalem) would certainly be among them. Check out their ministry websites listed under their Reviews.

To my friend and Publisher, **Sherrie Clark**, who makes *Storehouse Media Group* what it is. You have been a most patient and steadfast encouragement, graciously wanting this book to be the best it can be."

To some very **dear folks in Brady, Texas** who have been so welcoming to me.

Thank you also to my friend **Howard Laderman** for his Review who, though he is not at this time a believer in Jesus, nevertheless astutely perceived what takes place when the Holy Spirit anoints a person to write.

And to my wonderful daughters, **Ellen Cottrill** and **Jenny Lane** who are also my dearest friends!

And finally, among the others, this book opened with an enthusiastic Review by **Deborah Smith**, NE Regional AGLOW President, and ends in the Epilogue with what took place at a local AGLOW meeting where I was speaking when I read the final story, "Why Yeshua Wept," to them. So, in a sense, the book is bracketed in the gift of AGLOW. As a new believer, AGLOW women taught me how to walk with the Holy Spirit for which I remain grateful. Thank you AGLOW for the difference you make in the millions of lives of AGLOW members internationally and for your faithful support for Israel. [To find a local chapter go to: www.aglow.org.]

Foreword

Lonnie Lane has been an acquaintance, then a friend, and ultimately a co-laborer for the sake of Zion for more than thirty years. So, when I was asked to read her latest manuscript and make comments for publishing, of course I answered in the affirmative. "This is kind of different for me", she offered as she forwarded the file to my email account. I am used to her writing style of non-fiction as commentary or some revelation from her Bible, but this was to be different from the very conception.

The reader of this new fictional work will be taken into the untold thought life and experience of some of the best known, real life characters of the New Covenant Scriptures in order to explore what was happening between the lines of their very familiar and loved stories.

I must admit that I found myself being drawn into their (fictional) dialogues and experiences with an eagerness that quite surprised me. After all, we are people who are interested in other people, how they do life, what motivates them, etc., and in the discovery, we may find inspiration and hope for ourselves.

The portrayals of these very different persons and personalities I found to be intriguing and thoughtful. A very different look at the famous Samaritan woman at the well was one of my favorite stories as it challenged my casual opinion of her life and story to be a much more compassionate one that revealed my great lack of care about her or what had brought her to that well. I was reminded over and over again that these were just ordinary, everyday people, just like me, whose ordinary lives became extraordinary because of a divine interruption.

After reading this book I find myself longing for more divine interruptions and less of my own experiential wisdom to find the daily bread and the living water the Bible offers us. Thank you, Lonnie, for reminding me again that Yeshua makes life worth living, and...

Enjoying!

Paul Wilbur
www.Wilburministries.com

As an internationally acclaimed worship leader, whether Paul is leading worship before crowds of thousands in the Middle East, singing to packed soccer stadiums throughout Latin America, or bringing his anointed Messianic message directly to the people of Israel, he speaks the language of melody and meaning that reaches far beyond cultural, social and political borders to touch people directly with the love of God.

In addition to Paul's many recorded worship albums he is author of: *A King is Coming*; *Touching the Heart of God: Embracing the Calendar of the Kingdom*; and *Order in the Courts: Bringing Balance & Understanding in*

Expressive Praise & Worship. He has also served as the Executive Director of the International Messianic Jewish Alliance (IMJA).

Table of Contents

Notes to My Readers.. 1

Chapter 1: Levi's Taxing Dilemma................................... 5
Chapter 2: Vindication of the Samaritan Woman.......... 24
Chapter 3: Carpenters Are for Mending......................... 39
Chapter 4: Paralyzed No More 47
Chapter 5: Zaccheus' Short Story 53
Chapter 6: The Agony of Betrayal 56
Chapter 7: No Longer Just My Brother 66

Part II...91

Chapter 8: Why Yeshua Wept 93

Epilogue.. 109
About the Author... 112

Notes to My Readers

Welcome, friends. The stories you are about to read are fictional, although they are based on the Scriptural accounts of several people's lives as I pondered what it might have been like for them to have Yeshua invade their lives in the different ways that He did. It is my hope that the Holy Spirit had something to do with the insights in the stories.

I have attempted to put the characters and Yeshua Himself back into the Hebrew culture in which the events took place, including using their real Hebrew names in most cases. Yeshua was and still is Jesus' real Hebrew name and what He was called by everyone who knew Him. To write stories of those who knew Him then made it seem only right to address Him as they would have. I have done the same thing in giving most everyone else their Hebrew names – the names they would have called each other. My only exception is Peter in his story, as you will see.

Please be sure to read the footnotes when they appear as they will help bring some clarity.

Writing stories does take some wondering. For instance, have you ever wondered what it would have been like to be one of Yeshua's brothers or even His mother? Two of His brothers, James (Ya'acov) and Jude (Yehuda), have authored New Testament books. Their fiery-fervor makes me wonder about the kind of mother Mary (Miryam) must have been, to raise such sons. I am taking great liberty in presuming to speak for Ya'acov in telling his family's story. I'm trusting that the Lord has allowed me the liberty to share some of what that might have been like.

I have for years wanted to vindicate the Samaritan lady Yeshua met at their town well. How often has she been labeled as a loose or immoral woman? Yeshua said He did not come to judge but to save (John 12:47), so would He have judged her? Have some of us possibly misjudged His intentions in what He said to her? Could there have been a whole other set of circumstances in her life that He was referring to?

As some of the stories were originally written in loose poetic form (It is often how I process what I'm reading as I journal), listen for the rhyming that still somewhat remains. You may even find it fun to read chapters 3, 4 and 6, out loud for that reason, even reading them to someone else.

The events do not all follow how they are told in Scripture exactly. You will find that some parts of various stories are left out while others weave different parts, or even different characters, together. Maybe that's why the Gospels read as they do, as different perspectives of what took place. For the most part the stories just unfolded to me as I wrote them, as if the Holy Spirit was telling the stories to me. So, I take no credit in being resourceful or insightful. Even story-telling is a gift from the Lord.

PART 2 is set apart from the rest because I came to this one story much differently than the others. This was an experience with the Lord that is the most precious in its intimacy of any other revelation that He has shared with me. It is set apart because I feel it is worthy of a unique dignity and respect. It is more revelation than story-telling. It is the crowning glory of all the other stories included in this book.

It pieces different scenarios together that we might not have seen going together, but I am sharing it with you as I received it, one insight after the other. I do not presume that this is exactly what Yeshua was really experiencing. These insights came to me at a time when I needed to know that the Lord was truly *with* me in what I was experiencing. And so, I asked Him if, as Hebrews 4:15 says, Yeshua *really* experienced all things as we do, yet without sin. This story was His answer to me.

I would have preferred to keep the story between me and Him, but I feel that I am to include it here so that others will know how closely He can relate to us in our humanity. It also provides a surprise connecting of events at the end that may well have been what took place. Please resist the urge to read that story first so that you will know Yeshua as I hope you will find Him in the other stories before you come to that one.

I pray as you read through the book, you will find some of your own revelations of Him and that the Holy Spirit will make Yeshua and the experiences of those who knew Him more real to you as they did for me. To know Him more deeply is, after all, the goal and fulfillment in each of our lives for those of us who are truly His. It is also Abba's intention to make us conformed to Yeshua's likeness. For that, it seems we must continually come to know Him more deeply in the many aspects of our lives. May we each grow closer toward that goal day by day.

"Beloved, now we are children of God; and it has not yet been revealed what we shall be, but we know that when He is revealed, we shall be like Him, for we shall see Him as He is" (1 John 3:2).

Chapter 1
Levi's Taxing Dilemma

Matthew 5:46, 47 & 9:9

*"How little people know who think
that holiness is dull....
When one meets the real thing it's irresistible."*

- C.S. Lewis

Shalom, it's me, Levi.[1] You know, the man you hated, whom you considered a traitor to our people, the one most of you would never call a friend. Well, I don't blame you. But if you'll listen for a few minutes, I would like – no, I *need* to tell you my story. Because it's really a part of *our* story[2].

I grew up just like you, loving our people and loving our God. Someday, I thought, I'd make a difference for our people. As a young lad I had visions of driving out the

---

[1] The name Levi is Hebrew. In Greek his name is Matthew. He is the writer of the Gospel of Matthew.
[2] Levi, like most of us, did not expect Yeshua's invasion into his life and the challenges He would bring. Many of us can say the same thing. In that sense, it is *our* story.

Romans and freeing our people from their pagan tyranny over Israel. We would be a kingdom again like when David was king, when *Adonai* smiled upon us because He had smiled upon David. I didn't see myself becoming like David, of course. I didn't have that much *chutzpah*.[3] But I dreamed of one day joining with someone who could lead our people, of being part of his closest friends, helping him where I could. I wanted to make a difference. Well, don't most boys?

But my dreams changed when my *Abba's*[4] own dreams changed. He was a carpenter who had also done a lot of carving of smaller objects, things that are needed around the house. Ah, but he made them elegantly. He was really quite an artist. He made the handles of ladles into swans and wooden bowls that sat on feet like the paws of a lion. Our home was filled with such treasures.

He even made toys when I was a small boy that I would play with. Why, I had my own village, complete with people and animals. Then he began to do more carving than practical carpentry, often giving them away as gifts for weddings and special occasions and soon local folks were also buying them.

I remember how surprised we were when a Roman soldier came to our home wanting to buy a few of *Abba's* "pieces of art," as he called them. That was a turn-around for *Abba*. I remember him saying to my mother, "What if I could really sell these things to people outside of our

---

[3] *Chutzpah* is courage, guts.

[4] *Abba* is the name for Father or Daddy in Hebrew.

village? Like our village *shuk*⁵ there are others throughout the land. Maybe I could begin to sell them there."

And so, *Abba* began to carve more and once a month he would take a little trip to sell his creations elsewhere. He didn't sell them for too high a price as few Judeans could pay what that Roman had offered that day he came to our home. But still, as they say, it was a living.

Then someone said to *Abba*, "Your work is so good, you surely would have a market where there is more wealth and an appetite for such beautiful things." And so, *Abba* started thinking about this, and asking a lot of questions of merchants who would come through our Galilean town. We were, after all, on a trade route where merchants and even caravans came through on their way to elsewhere.

Sometimes *Abba* sold his wares to those merchants who laughed and said how much more money they could sell them for where they were going. Pretty soon *Abba* began to wonder if he too shouldn't be selling his carvings where they were going. The idea of the *kesef* ⁶ he would earn spurred him on to more carvings and less carpentry to the extent that we were beginning to feel the lack of needed *kesef* in our own home. But now *Abba* had a vision. He would go where the *kesef* was!

He worked very diligently for several weeks, finding the lumber, paring it down to bare wood and carving and

---

⁵ A *shuk* is an outdoor market in Israel where food and all manner of things are sold.

⁶ *Kesef* is Hebrew for money.

fitting pieces together so that one part fit just perfectly into another and soon he had amassed quite a collection of beautifully carved pieces. Some were useful utensils while others were less useful but quite extraordinary in their beauty.

One I particularly liked was a small box with a fitted lid that he had carved a scene into of trees and a stream. He made one like it for my mother, though I don't remember what she kept in it. And he made one somewhat like it for me, though a bit longer and flatter.

At first, I wondered what I would keep in it, but a few weeks before *Abba* was going to join a group of merchants on their journey to wherever it is merchants go, he took me aside and presented me with one of his very special carving knives. I was about twelve then and old enough that he had taught me to handle a knife properly. For that next two weeks, he kept me near him, showing me how to use it without cutting myself and how to arc the knife just so to pare away the wood to go with the grain, and when to apply more pressure to go a bit deeper to carve a shape into the wood.

While it was only days that we were working together, it was not long before I began to feel the wonder of that knife in my hand, and like God, I was creating! I marveled at how my own hands, like those of my *Abba,* were able to turn a dead piece of wood into something that appeared to have a life of its own in what it represented. My dreams changed that week. I would become a wood carver like my *Abba.* I told him so and he hugged me close.

The day he left, he loaded up our donkey with two big satchels my mother had sewn for him out of strong cloth she got from the tent maker in our village. A smaller one held food and a skin of watered-down wine. The bigger one held his carvings. I was excited for him and looked forward to the *kesef* he would bring home and to the gift from the world outside of our village that he promised to bring me. *Ima*[7] didn't seem as excited. She seemed sad, or worried, I could tell, but she put on a happy face and kissed him and said a prayer that *Adonai* would keep him safe and bring him back to us soon.

With the lead for the donkey in hand, he turned one more time for a hug from *Ima* and one from me, and off he went to meet with the merchant caravan waiting on the other side of our village. Just like that, my *Abba* walked out of our lives into another life we could only try to imagine. And he never came back.

Oh yes, we waited for his return, talking together about what he would bring back with him and what we would buy with the *kesef* he would bring. But as the weeks went on, our waiting turned into a deep sadness that he might never return. To make matters worse, though he was careful to put all the *kesef* he could in a jar he had carved for *Ima* to buy whatever we needed until his return, it was soon all but gone as was the store of food that had been prepared or purchased. It was not too long before *Ima* and I were on the verge of poverty.

Ima took in sewing and doing what other women didn't want to do and made some money, and at twelve I became a man. Not because I had a bar mitzvah, but

---

[7] *Ima*, pronounced Eemah means mother in Hebrew.

because I went to work to support us, doing odd jobs wherever I could find them and trying to be industrious and think up new ways to make myself worthy of being hired by someone to do something. Anything. Meanwhile, my carving knife stayed under my bed in the box *Abba* had carved for me and soon I forgot all about it.

Somehow the years went by and we no longer – or at least I no longer looked down the path leading to our home, nor did I scan the horizon with hopeful eyes to see if *Abba* was returning. We never found out what happened to him. We had heard of bandits who cared more for what they could take from merchants or ordinary men carrying their wares than for the lives of those to whom the treasures belonged. *Ima* would on occasion mention what she feared had happened to him, but soon even those thoughts she kept to herself.

As for me, even though I had loved my *Abba*, I became somewhat bitter that he had left us and even more that he had left us penniless. Now my dreams were to take care of my mother, of course, but also that I would never be in this position again, once I found a way out of it. There had to be a way to be prosperous and earn enough money so that neither I nor *Ima* would ever be poor again.

I would have my own family one day, and I would see to it that we had a fine house, one like those I had seen in Sephoris where the traders went to buy and sell their treasures. Those were real houses with rooftop gardens and stairs leading up to them, and several rooms and sometimes even a pool in the middle to bathe. I had traveled there once with *Abba* to deliver some of the furniture he used to make and had been inside one of those houses. My eyes had widened with the splendor of it all.

Now my dream was to live like that. When I first aspired to have such a house I would have added, "*Adonai* willing," to my dream. But as time went on, my ambition stirred within me and *Adonai* had less and less to do with it. I would just have to make my own way. After all, *Adonai* had let us get into this poverty so why should I trust Him to bring me wealth?

The first years I did odd jobs to earn some of the money that kept us going. But then, over time I found ways to make myself useful to the Roman soldiers that were everywhere in Judea. They tended to spend their money for what they wanted more easily than Judeans did for the basics they needed. Soon I was not only running errands for them, but I was finding out information for them and… well, one thing led to another and then, having made the acquaintance of some of the Roman soldiers who oversaw various aspects of their imposing presence among our people, as I grew into a man I was offered the job of a tax collector.

My immediate thought was that I would be acting for Rome. Wasn't that being a traitor to my people? Many had even lost their properties only to become as serfs to Rome because of the required taxes.[8] But, then I began to rationalize that someone had to do it. Why not I who would be fairer to our people than the Romans by not

---

[8] Taxes could be up to 50%. The New Testament doesn't really address the depth of oppression Rome held over the people.

charging them a higher rate than what was due? A percentage above the tax was to be mine so I could set it at whatever price I chose. The Romans didn't care what I charged so long as they got their cut.

My initial intentions were to be as honorable as I could while still earning what would be a reasonable surcharge for doing the job. But soon it was too easy to add a few more *shekels*[9] here and there. It wasn't long before I began to see how much my own people resented me. I knew they hated the presence of the Romans altogether. I did too. We all did. But soon I was seen as if I was one of *them* and not one with my people.

It took just a little while for me to realize this but soon the reality of it began to affect my own thinking. I had a right to earn a living doing what I was doing, didn't I? I managed to maintain at least a cordial relationship with several of the men in my village, but they only talked with me when they came to pay their taxes, and even then, I knew they pretended that I was still one of them so that I wouldn't raise their interest rate.

When our paths crossed in the otherwise busyness of life in our village, they lowered their heads or looked elsewhere as if they didn't see me. I was being ostracized. And it was all because of money. Soon I stopped going to synagogue even on the holy days because standing there with a *tallit*[10] around my shoulders, while no one would even stand near me, made me feel as if the *tallit* was a

---

[9] *Shekels* are coins of various amounts used as money.

[10] *Tallit* (pronounced tah-LEET) is a fringed prayer shawl.

weight I wanted to be free of. And so, I left not only the synagogue but in time, *Adonai* [11] as well.

Yet, I did find a wife. A pretty woman, who had lost her first husband to the Romans when they indiscriminately murdered a few men just to keep order in an incident which had occurred between some soldiers and several Judeans. As quickly as it takes to thrust a *gladius*[12] into someone's body, his life came to an abrupt end. She shared my bitterness toward the Romans but was happy enough to enjoy the money that now bought us one of the houses such as I had longed for when I was a young boy.

While most of my *kesef* admittedly now came from the Jews and not the Romans, in time I lost sight of that and was more intent on supporting the lifestyle we had come to enjoy. And after all, wasn't I now employing a few Hebrew servants, bringing some income to them too?

And so, this is how our lives went. I would go to my tax collection booth every day but *Shabbat*[13] since no one would come on *Shabbat* anyway. My booth was in the middle of town where the required taxes would be paid. I kept scrupulous records of who paid how much, and for what, and when their taxes were due.

---

[11] *Adonai* (Ah-doan-EYE) is Hebrew for Lord, the name that was used for YHVH; for God.

[12] A *gladius* is short Roman sword which varied in weight between 2 to 3 pounds, 9 ounces.

[13] *Shabbat* (pronounced Shah-BAHT) is the Sabbath which is always on a Saturday.

I was no longer without friends as in time, especially once I had acquired a standing of my own in the world of businessmen, such as they were. These included several other tax collectors and people of various 'occupations' who were also as disdained by the Judeans as I was. But no matter, we had our own *chavurah*.[14] We shared a sense of belonging to one another, mostly based on how we made our money though, of course, we talked about other things besides our business dealings.

Then, on a day which began like any other, a crowd of local folks[15] gathered near the center of town. It was an unusual occurrence for a weekday when people were generally busy with their everyday lives. From where I sat at the opening of my booth I could easily watch what was happening there. Leaning my elbows on the shelf where business usually took place, I watched. A Man was speaking, standing to one side of the crowd, facing them. From where He stood, I could see His face and wondered what He was saying that people evidently found so interesting.

Since no one came to pay their taxes that day, I directed my attention to see if I could hear why this ordinary looking Man had attracted such a crowd. As He continued to speak His voice carried further than I would have expected and so, despite having only half an interest, I listened since I had nothing else to do. But it

---

[14] *Chavurah* (Hav-or-AH) is Hebrew for a fellowship or friendship group.

[15] The word for "local people" has often been translated in our English bibles as "multitudes."

was not long before I wondered where in the world this Man got those ideas, or why people were even bothering to listen to Him. He sure had a different way of looking at things. When He began to say things having to do with money, I paid more attention to what He was saying.

"*If anyone wants to sue you and take away your tunic, let him have your cloak also.*"[16] At that statement, I strangely felt like I wanted to wrap the new cloak I had recently bought around me as if to hold onto it. I tried to figure out the reason behind what He had just said. Why would He be telling them this? Give someone more than they're asking for in a legal battle? That made no sense. Then I thought I had it figured out. Oh, He must mean to avoid getting into a legal battle.

I decided He was offering them a shrewd business tactic. Give the man what he wants rather than risk court costs and a judge deciding against you. Personalizing what He was saying, I thought I could give my cloak away and just as easily buy a new cloak, but I was ignoring that not everyone has that luxury or that a man's cloak may be all he has to keep him warm. I didn't think of that then. But I was listening more intently now, curious as to where He was going with all this talk.

"*And whoever compels you to go one mile, go with him two. Give to him who asks you, and from him who wants to borrow from you do not turn away.*" Borrow? Sure, some people had wanted to borrow from me, ironically to pay their taxes, and sure, I lent them the

---

[16] This whole dialog is found in Matthew 5:40-48.

kesef to pay their taxes – at added interest. I wasn't in business to give away money, but to gain it. But what's this being compelled by someone? No one compels us but the Romans.

I remembered times when as a lad I was compelled to do things for them, run errands for them, or do work that they didn't want to do as I got older. I was certainly compelled by them back then. But now this Man is saying to do double of what they're asking? This is crazy talk. I wondered just how far He would be willing to go to fulfill His own words if He was ever asked to go the extra mile in His own life. Or was this just bravado He would never have to live out? He sounds like a philosopher. He's full of good ideas that have no feet on the ground in reality. This Man is surely seeing things from a strange perspective, that's for sure. But still, I kept on listening.

"You have heard that it was said, 'You shall love your neighbor and hate your enemy.'" Right, I know that one. My fellow Jews are being true to that verse, for many of them see me as their enemy and they hate me. They don't realize they could have far more stolen from them than I was charging them, much less than some of the other tax collectors I knew.

"I say to you, love your enemies, bless those who curse you, do good to those who hate you, and pray for those who spitefully use you and persecute you...."

Hold on there, now that's really crazy talk. Loving your enemies is contrary to everything I and every other Hebrew stood for. Hating the Romans is surely how *Adonai* Himself must feel about them and every other enemy of Israel. Doesn't He? My fellow Jews may hate me, but they aren't really hating *me,* only what I was doing that cost them money. But the Romans, they are truly hated, and justifiably. The whole of Israel has been under their pagan influence and their military control for decades.

Oh, for the days when David ruled! We all longed for those days again. Still, I continued to try and make sense out of what this Man was saying, still wondering why everyone bothered to listen to him. Then it occurred to me that I was still listening to Him too.

I turned my attention back to what He was in the middle of saying: "... *that you may be sons of your Father in heaven, for He makes His sun rise on the evil and on the good and sends rain on the just and on the unjust."* These words pierced my heart with the startling question of whether indeed I was one of the just or the unjust. Certainly, I wasn't an evil person. There were some I might have considered as such, and certainly, those Romans were. But this had to do with justice and for the first time, I wondered if my added taxes also added to the injustice of the Romans who taxed us for living on our own land.

Plus, I had never really thought of *Adonai* as giving rain and all else we need in this life, let alone to both the evil and the good. But which was I? I knew I was certainly not on very good terms with Him. Nor did I think of *Adonai* as a Father other than of Him tending to disappear and leave you on your own the way my own father had.

"For if you love those who love you, what reward have you?" I let my thoughts briefly consider what He just said

about love. Yes, I love my wife and my dear *Ima* who still lives with me. But I don't look for any reward for loving them, if the truth be told.... Funny that word should come to me, truth. When do I ever think about that concept? I suppose loving them is kind of a reward in itself. Yes, they love me back but is that what this Man is talking about? He couldn't be talking about there being some monetary reward for loving others, could He?

My thoughts were interrupted when He said: *"Do not even the tax collectors do the same?"* His words shot across the village square as if He was saying them directly to me. And for a second, I could have sworn He looked over the crowd to right where I was sitting and caught my eye for a second while I was watching all this from the window of my booth. Why would I even think such a thing? He now had my full attention though. He couldn't be talking about me, could He? He couldn't be! What's more, he's using love and tax collectors in the same discussion. I was certainly not accustomed to the two being discussed in connection with one another. Maybe He's out of touch with what's really going on here. All these thoughts came tumbling after one another in my mind and before I could even begin to sort them out He continued speaking.

"And if you greet your brothers only, what do you do more than others?" I was relieved that He was no longer talking about tax collectors, but then I thought that if I warmly greeted anyone it was only those with whom I was like-minded, and if any of them were as brothers to me or even some as sisters, it was because we were all on the outside of the accepted social mainstream of our village.

I usually greeted them only and no one else, preferring not to look at anyone else eye to eye, I now realized. How was I not conscious of this before? Well, it was mutual. They didn't consider me as a brother either. This Man had just put His verbal finger on how separated I was from everyone else I had grown up among, the very people whom I had once thought of as my people. How did I get so far from them?

I hadn't planned to. I had never questioned being a part of them growing up. My family was always with all the other families in those days. But somehow things were different after *Abba* disappeared. It became too painful to be with everyone else at family times or even in the synagogue after he was gone. Little by little things changed and now those I would consider like family were those whom everyone else considered enemies and sinners. It was a hard yoke to carry though I always silently pretended it wasn't as I busied myself with living a somewhat lucrative life.

But now, this Man, whoever He was, was portraying tax collectors as being those whose only motive is for the reward of the *kesef* that they gain. Have I been reduced to that kind of a person? For the first time it occurred to me that my own father had gone in pursuit of wealth and had lost his life in the process. Had I too lost my life in another sense as I also sought wealth? Outside I thought I looked like I was a success in many ways, but who was I inside, in the place where I was the man I really was? Who had I become where it really mattered, in my heart?

In time the Man left, being followed by a group of other men while the rest of the crowd ambled back to their daily lives. But their conversations were not what they had been before He came. As days went on I could overhear all kinds of discussions from my tax booth in the square, and often when someone would come to me to pay their taxes, they seemed to have a different attitude toward me. They greeted me as if they once again knew me as someone who was one of them. "*Shalom, Levi. Mah'shlomcha? Ha kol tov?*" - Hello Levi, how are you? Everything good?" as if they actually cared. Asking me how I am is the same as asking literally "How is my peace?"[17] While it is the usual greeting, since that Man had spoken, whatever peace I did have before, such as it was, was now replaced by rethinking over and over what He had said.

I couldn't seem to make His words go away. I hadn't been plagued with such self-doubts before. Now I felt an angst inside I didn't remember feeling ever before. I kept having thoughts of when I first began to work for the Romans. I did have to resolve a conflict within myself then. But survival won out and I left my conscience behind somewhere in order to support my mother and in time it disappeared altogether in order to build a new lifestyle for myself.

Now the conscience that had been lying dormant somewhere inside seemed stirred to the point of discomfort. I responded by asking my inquirers how their peace was in return. A cordial greeting, but I wondered if what that Man had to say was the reason I was now being

---

[17] That phrase, *Mah'shlomcha*, does actually translate as "How is your peace" and is the usual greeting in Israel even today.

regarded more warmly. Were they as affected by what He said as much as I was? Had they considered that I was the enemy they now had to go the extra mile with? At one time not long ago, I wouldn't have thought twice about taking someone's cloak instead of money they didn't have, if it came to that. But for the first time, the cover on what I now realized was my greed had been ripped off and I felt as if my conscience had been stripped naked. The Man's words continued to reverberate through my mind as the days went on.

Something else also stirred within me. Lying awake at night next to my sleeping wife, again and again, I considered what that Man's words meant to me until it seemed like they were etched into my soul. A memory began to the surface as I recalled when I was much younger, in the days when I had thought that someday I would make a difference for our people. I had longed for another like King David to come to our people again. I remembered those days I had day-dreamed about becoming one of the men like David had alongside of him, someone as godly and brave as David, who could save our people from all that threatens us. I remembered thinking how I would follow him as one of his faithful ones, helping him where I could and together we would make a difference even to all Israel.

Each time the memory surfaced as it did again and again, I increasingly had the feeling that there was some destiny involved in that memory. But what could it be? I had just come to see how evil and greed had taken hold of my life and now I didn't know how to get out of it, even if I wanted to. Did I want to? What would I do if I did? I was entirely perplexed as to how one afternoon I overheard the words of some Man I didn't even know and ever since my whole life seemed upside down.

It was about then that I had the most unusual feeling that what I needed to do was what I hadn't done for over two decades, and that was to talk with *Adonai.* Isn't that what David did when he was stressed, fearful when facing his enemies and even when he had sinned greatly, feeling that not only had he sinned against a person, he had sinned against *Adonai?* After all, the standard of righteousness is His.

I wasn't sure I even knew how to pray anymore. But finally, right there in my tax collector's booth where I now saw that I sinned almost daily by being dishonest and greedy, I closed the window and in the semi-darkness of that little booth, I began to tell *Adonai* that I was sorry I had become the man I had. I asked Him to forgive me for ignoring Him for years, for acting as if He wasn't even there and didn't matter. I asked Him to forgive me for my greed and hard-heartedness, and disregard for my fellow Jews. Once I began to let this all out, one thing after another came to me and at some point, I began to cry, something I hadn't done in years.

I poured out my heart till I was wrung out and exhausted and had not one thing more to say except to add, "*Adonai,* please tell me what I'm to do now because I surely can't continue to do what I have been doing. But I don't know how to get out of it. Or what I would even do then?"

Now that I had a new set of thoughts I felt a peace I had forgotten existed. I had the sense that somehow

Adonai was going to show me, and I would know it when He did.

Two days later I saw that same Man walking into the town square. I wondered if I would be able to hear Him this time if He addressed a group of people again. But then He seemed to be making His way toward my tax booth. He wasn't going to pay some kind of tax, was He? But when He came up to the booth, He called me by my name. How did He even know my name? I was stunned and speechless as He smiled and looked into my eyes which, no doubt, were wide open with wonder at what was happening. Then He reached into the window and put His hand on my arm and looked at me with eyes that seemed as if they had nothing hidden. I felt as if He was looking deep into my soul, and He simply said, "*Levi, follow Me.*" And I did.

Chapter 2
Vindication of the Samaritan Woman

John 4:4-42

"We never know what destiny will meet us in the mundane."

-Anonymous

What could be more ordinary than a trek to the local well to draw water – again! In the heat, walking the dusty trail, she made her way in the heat of the noonday sun. Despite the fact that this very well was one from which Jacob himself had drawn water for his family and his animals, a fact which often awed her, there seemed no glory in it today. She absent-mindedly shifted the empty water jug, bearing the weight of it from one hip to the other as she began, once again, to rehearse the litany of the years of her life, wondering why it had all unfolded as it did. She didn't always allow those thoughts to come, but they seemed to come unbidden today, and so she let them come.

Perhaps *Adonai* had lost sight of her. Did He even know she existed? Perhaps He was displeased with her as it certainly seemed so. Or worse, she thought, as her brows furrowed, and her mind turned to the question that so often haunted her. She and her people were half-breed Jews, with as much Assyrian blood as Hebrew blood flowing through their veins. Had *Adonai* turned away from them the way the Hebrews had? They never worshipped in the temple in Jerusalem as the Jews did, having declared their own place of worship where they lived in Samaria. But did *Adonai* even hear their prayers? He certainly didn't seem to hear hers.

How many times had she taken this trail to the well and wondered these same thoughts? She wondered also if it could be possible that *Adonai* even knew how much she longed to know Him? Soon her thoughts turned to reminiscing, as they so often did, of the years that added up to the picture of her life, wondering again and again how all that had taken place had actually happened to her. Her frown turned into a smile as she remembered the happiest time in her young life. It had all seemed so perfect once, and she couldn't have been any more at peace in the joy of her marriage to David. Walking automatically now as her thoughts drifted back in time she once again let the memories make themselves known, one by one with each step she took.

She and her David had played together as children and had grown up learning the ways of the world around them together, delighting in playing with the animals both their families owned, exploring the world around them, enjoying the changes in the seasons, and pretending they were grown up as children do and talking about what life would surely hold for them when they grew up.

So, it was quite natural that they would be married one day. They had planned it even as children. And the day finally came when he was her precious bridegroom and she his beautiful bride. She smiled again, unaware that she had, as she recalled again how tender he was with her on the first night of their marriage as they clung to one another surprised by the joy *Adonai* had created in the union between a man and a woman. In the morning, and often afterward, they had looked into each other's eyes where they had seen such hope, such joy, and such expectation of a long life together.

There would be children, many of them, girls who would look like her and boys who would grow to be strong and handsome like their *Abba*. But it was not meant to be as just months after their wedding he was ripped out of her life in one brief moment of carelessness on someone's else's part. Life had been crushed out of him, and with it, her own life, and everything she loved or ever wanted was crushed along with him.

She took a deep breath of the hot noon air as if to draw in some of the life she had lost when she lost David, as she continued her thoughts, remembering, remembering, remembering with each step. When David had died, before she could even begin to find any light in life again, his family had arranged for her to be married to his brother Daniel in the way that *Torah* prescribes for women in the family who lose their husbands.[18] The idea behind it is merciful, and she was grateful that David's family who,

---

[18] A Deuteronomy 25:5-10 says that when a man dies, his brother should marry the deceased's wife and bring forth children in the name of her first husband, so his generational line will continue.

even in their own grief, showed concern for her well-being. Daniel was good-looking enough and a pleasant man, only somewhat resembling David. She had known him from childhood also. But how could she give herself to him? He was not her beloved. But neither could he, knowing the love that existed between her and his brother, expect it of her. And so, she lived a childless life on the sidelines of her two husbands' family, never really feeling like she belonged as she had when David still lived and there was the expectation of a growing family. Nor was she ever free of the burden of the grief she wore like heavy shawl upon her shoulders.

She stumbled upon a small rock, not having paid attention to her steps as she walked. She would have to be more careful to balance the jug on her hip lest it come crashing to the ground. Even with that distraction, her thoughts continued to come one after another as she made her way to the well, thoughts that seemed to want to make themselves known more than usual today.

Then there was Yosef, dear Yosef. Such a joy that man was. Even from the beginning, he seemed to be able to pierce the darkness and make her laugh at the silliest things. He often came to visit the family and in time they began to talk with one another. Though he was somewhat older than she, she felt quite comfortable with him. Yosef was a widower whose wife had died in childbirth along with their first child a number of years ago. And Yosef had never remarried. He had often been a visitor to her family, enough so that he sometimes seemed a part of them. In time, though it was inappropriate for her to be speaking with him privately as she was Daniel's wife, she remembered how she always enjoyed his company when he came to visit, and if she had dared to think so then, he seemed to enjoy hers as well.

Then one very unexpected day Daniel and her father-in-law asked her to come and be with them in the garden as they had something they wanted to talk to her about. Both men seemed very uncomfortable which made her feel more nervous than they appeared to be, but finally, the issue was presented to her. Since she and Daniel had never consummated the marriage – an embarrassing enough issue, especially to discuss with one's father-in-law – and since it seemed as if it would not become a real marriage, which they hastened to add they both understood under the circumstances of David's death, but so that Daniel could go on to a marriage in which he could one day have children, they proposed an annulment of the marriage vows. The shock of it alarmed her immediately. Her first thought was that they were abandoning her. Where would she live? How would she support herself?

But her fears were immediately redirected as her father-in-law continued to say that their friend Yosef the widower had come to him to propose that if, as he suspected, the marriage to Daniel was *Levirate*[19] only, meaning legal according to *Torah* but not one of a loving union, that the marriage be annulled, and she be given to Yosef in marriage. She could not have been more stunned and had sat speechless for long enough for both men to clear their throats and ask her to think about it.

---

[19] The name of the Deuteronomy 25:1-10 marriage described above.

And so, it was that she became the wife of Yosef. And she found a measure of happiness, such as it was, for the first time since David had died. Yosef was good to her and a delight to live with. He brought her little thoughtful gifts and was so helpful to her in so many ways. But since he was considerably older than she, he often needed her help as well. In fact, she sometimes felt more like his nurse than his wife. And though they were intimate with one another, no children came. Then after several years of pleasantness and enjoying being there for one another, she came home one day from the market to find Yosef had fallen and was unable to get up by himself. He had lain there on the stone tile floor waiting for her to come home and help him get up.

But he had never really recovered as the fall seemed to have happened due to some weakness within him. Despite months of nursing him and the local doctor coming frequently to check on him, in time, one day, Yosef was gone. Just like that. He was with her no more. Her sense of loss was paralyzing for a long while and she missed him terribly.

As is normal in Jewish families, siblings and their wives often shared the family home where they had grown up and so it was that she and Yosef shared the house with his brother Nathaniel and his wife Miryam. Now that Yosef was gone, they were so gracious to keep her included in the family, never once even mentioning that she no longer belonged. Their children were now grown with children of their own, though they visited often, filling the house with a noisy joy as only children can. The children treated her as the Aunt they always loved. The relationship between them was an easy one and she and Miryam had become devoted to one another as if they had been sisters all their lives.

But in time Miryam, the one woman she had so fondly come to know as her sister-in-law and friend, also passed away, adding to the sorrow that so unrelentingly permeated her life. Still, life had to go on, and so in time, she developed a lifestyle of going on in numbness. But now, here she and Nathaniel were in this situation that was against the ways of *Torah* and their people – an unmarried man and woman living in the same house. Something had to be done. She feared the outcome.

But Nathaniel, as a faithful *Torah* follower, did what he knew was right and made a proposal to her of marriage. Now that it was only the two of them living in the household, honorable man that he was, and wishing to secure a legal name and home for her, he made her the offer. He had been quite fond of her and she of him, but only as brother and sister-in-law, neither ever considering the other in terms of marriage. When he approached her with the idea, as they had always had an easiness between them, they were able to address this kind of fondness between them as one that did not include a marital attachment.

Still, the situation seemed to make logical sense. And so, they were married though each retained their part of the house and they simply continued to live pretty much as they had. Until the day she found that life had fled from him too. Death had become all too familiar to her and she began to wonder what the end of her own life would be like.

Even so, several years slipped by and she continued to live in the house alone. As the family had been fairly well off, she suffered no lack even as a woman on her own. Still, she knew it was frowned upon in the village. She could feel the tongues wagging about all her misfortune so that she began to go to the well, the usual village gossiping place, when few others were around.

She expected that she would forever remain alone. Until that is, she realized that Eliezer, a man she had known for years seemed to be around more often. He arranged for various reasons to be nearby, often walking her home from synagogue, or being available to be there when she needed help with something. On occasion, he invited her to have dinner with him and his children and she would bring a dish they all seemed to enjoy more than his cooking.

The plain fact soon became evident: Though they were no longer young, still his children needed a mother. She began to help with them, cooking meals for them, or tending to them when he couldn't be available, listening to the stories of what their days were like, and even mending their clothes. She had always loved children and grieved over the loss of those she never had. In time, they fell into an easy way of life and he invited her to move into his home, so she could be there whenever the children needed her. She would have her own quarters, of course. This, she reasoned, was her one chance to be as a mother even if it was to someone else's children. Soon the children began to regard her as a natural part of their family.

She would never replace their own mother, of course, but still, they began to look to her in the ways in which children look to their mother. And though she and Eliezer weren't married[20] now she finally had children to look after – and to love. She often reminded herself of one of the psalms which said, *"He causes the childless woman to live at home happily as a mother of children."*[21] That she lived with him as more of a nurse[22] for his children than anything else was regarded by her and by Eliezer as something that was a blessing for each of them. She had almost every responsibility of a wife, though none of the security or the identity of one.

She accepted her fate, grateful for the love of the children and the friendship of Eliezer. Still, it did trouble her that one day the children would be grown, and then what? It seemed she would never again know the tenderness and the sense of really belonging to a loving husband. Was there ever to be any lasting security in her life? Wasn't there a security that could be known in *Adonai* that, for reasons she never could grasp, she had somehow also missed? This had remained a perennial question to her, one that she doubted would ever be answered.

Finally, she arrived at the well, and much to her surprise, a Hebrew Man was sitting on the shallow wall of the well. Her first thought was that He seemed to be waiting for someone. But who would a Hebrew be waiting for in Samaria? It would be highly irregular. She had known immediately that He was a Hebrew by His dress and the fringes that peeked out from

---

[20] I have made Eliezer as if he was her 5th 'husband' to whom she was not really married. By now I expect you get the idea of how her life may have gone in terms of loosing husbands.

[21] Psalm 113:9.

[22] A nurse would be like a nanny today.

beneath His outer garment. Was it safe to be near Him, she wondered, slowing her approach to the well, not sure if she should come near or not?

As casually as if it wasn't against custom for a Jew to speak to a Samaritan, let alone a strange man to a woman He didn't know, the Man said to her in what sounded by His tone like more of a request than a demand, "*Give me a drink.*" She took the risk to raise her head and looked into His face to see if she could read His intent. Could she trust this Man, or should she flee? Surprised, she found she was met with kindness as He gazed back at her with an openness not known between Hebrews and Samaritans.

Still confused as to what to do she lowered her head to think. But as she glanced up again at His face, the fear she had first felt melted away and she responded timidly by asking, "How is it that you, a Hebrew, ask me for a drink?" She had a cup tied to her sash, but she was pretty sure a Hebrew wouldn't drink from the cup of a Samaritan anyway who they would likely consider unclean. But it was a hot day and it was already noon. He must be very thirsty, she thought. And so, she drew water from the well, filled her cup and then tentatively handed it to Him.

Smiling at her, He reached out a broad and strong hand, which she much later would find was the hand of a carpenter and took the cup from her. Swallowing the last of the water in the cup He handed it back to her, wiping His wet lips with the back of His hand. Then He began to speak to her as if He was picking up in the middle of a conversation they had already been having. "*Everyone who drinks of this water,*" He said, "*will thirst again but whoever drinks of the water that I will give him shall never thirst.*"

Never thirst, she wondered. How can that be? Oh, to never have to come to the well day after day," she thought and then ventured to ask Him how she could obtain this water.

He didn't give her the answer she was hoping He would, but He continued to say, *"The water that I will give him will become in him a well of water springing up to eternal life."* For the first time in her life, it occurred to her that what she had considered her connection to God, that Ya'acov[23] had known *Adonai* and had used this well to water his flocks, was in fact only a story of how others had known *Adonai* in the past. It didn't make *Adonai* any closer to her. Or for that matter, make her any closer to Him.

Was there something that she could learn of *Adonai* from this Hebrew Man today, she wondered? If so, then she wanted what He seemed to be saying. She wanted this water He spoke of. At that moment she realized that her own thirst was to know *Adonai* herself in a way that far exceeded recalling how Jacob and his sons and their flocks drank from this well all those centuries ago.

Being sure to speak to Him with the respect she now felt He somehow deserved, even as a dreaded Hebrew, she said, *"Sir, give me this water, so I will not be thirsty nor have to come all the way here to draw."* Then He said to her the one thing she would never have wanted to hear from a prophet of *Adonai* as she began to suspect He might be. *"Go, call your husband and come here,"* He said.

Pain shot through her heart at that moment. Hadn't she just gone through remembering all that had transpired

---

[23] Jacob

regarding the men in her life? Dare she tell this Man the truth, this one who seemed to know so much? He hadn't said it unkindly. Could He possibly know her truths even if she didn't tell Him? Despite all she had been through, the truth was, that at this time, there was no one she could truly call her husband even if she lived in the home of a man with his family. The moments went by as hours as shame washed over her until she was barely able to whisper, "*I have no husband.*"

Then very gently, as if reaching into her heart with a compassion she had never known from any man, even her David, He began to speak to her further of what she had just recited to herself on her trip to the well. Although He said it gently He ended by saying, "*You have correctly said, 'I have no husband' for you have had five husbands, and the one whom you now have is not your husband. This you have said truly.*"

She stood there staring at Him, having no idea what to say next, not knowing what He expected of her. There was no judgment, either in His voice or the way He looked at her. Stunned that He would know all this, and even more so that there was no condemnation coming from Him, another thought came to her like a flash of lightning on a dark night. Could this Man possibly be the Messiah we have been waiting for all these many generations that He would know so much about her? Could it possibly be?

If so, perhaps He would answer a question that she had been longing to know the answer to for years. She desperately wanted to know whether her fellow Samaritans were worshipping on a mountain that *Adonai* approved of. Was it on their mountain or the mountain of Jerusalem as the Jews believed where *Adonai* could hear their prayers? It had long troubled her that her people were worshipping on the wrong mountain and she often tried to imagine what that would mean if so. This might be her one opportunity to find the truth.

Rather than acknowledging the list of her own life experiences and taking a risk at being seen as a foolish woman she began to ask what she had for so long wanted to be answered but had no one to ask. "*Sir,*" she said, again respectfully, "*I perceive that You are a prophet. Our people worship on this mountain, but you Jews say that Jerusalem is the place where men ought to worship.*" She hadn't actually asked a question, but He seemed to know what was on her heart and began to answer her question more clearly than she would have ever expected.

"*Woman, believe Me,*" He said as He stood up for the first time and opened His arms wide as if He was welcoming the world. A bit alarmed she did not expect He would respond to her with such fervor, nor did she have any idea of what He was about to say, but she had the distinct sense that whatever it was He said, she would believe Him.

"*An hour is coming,*" He continued, "*when neither on this mountain nor in Jerusalem will you worship the Father. You worship what you do not know; we worship what we know, for salvation is from the Jews. But…*" and He seemed to emphasize His "But" as He held up a finger to make the point He was about to make, "*… an hour is coming, and now is, when the true worshipers will worship the Father in spirit and truth; for such people the Father seeks to be His worshipers. Adonai is spirit, and those who worship Him must worship in spirit and truth.*"

She wasn't sure she understood all He had just said to her, but she indeed had the sense that His words carried a promise of more truth she would come to know. What she did grasp was that the Father wanted her worship! That He was even looking for worshippers, not based on whether they were Jews or Samaritans, or where they lived or where they even worshipped, but on whether they had hearts that truly wished to worship Him.

A guarded joy began to flicker inside of her as immediately another question began to burn in her heart to ask Him. So, she took the risk to press Him further and said, almost breathlessly, "*I know that Messiah is coming, and when that One comes, He will declare all things to us.*" She wasn't sure she had even asked a question. But with much joy reflected in His face and looking at her with the eyes of a Man who had nothing hidden in them the way most men did, He simply said, "*I who speak to you am He.*"

Silence filled the air. His statement seemed to capture even the attention of the birds in the trees, silencing them too with the same awe that stunned her. Her mind spun with the thought that this Man sitting on the edge of her well could possibly be the Messiah. He had actually come. And He had come to her! Before she could even begin to grasp the full significance of what had just taken place, or even consider how to respond to the astounding significance of His words, a group of other Hebrew men suddenly arrived. They evidently knew Him well and though He had spoken to her without any animosity, they looked at her with that same look of disdain that Hebrews look at Samaritans, causing her to want to flee from their presence.

Before they could ask what He was doing speaking to a Samaritan woman, she dashed off toward town, fleeing from the men who had just come, while overflowing with wanting to share what had just happened and whom she had met. Surely, they all had to know. It wasn't until she arrived breathlessly at home and began to tell Eliezer that she realized she had left her water jug at the well. She felt sure it would be there when she returned for it, hoping He too would still be there. It didn't take too long to gather their small town to meet Him.

If this Man was indeed the Messiah, they all needed to know that finally, and even to them as Samaritans, He was making Himself known. She knew deep within herself, that nothing would ever be the same again. *Adonai* had not only known her, He had sent His Messiah to the least of all persons, to her, a Samaritan woman without a husband.

As she ran into town, Eliezer slightly behind her, she had the overwhelming desire that what she wanted more than anything now was for the whole world, the world He seemed to have opened His arms to, to know that Messiah had finally come. And He had come, not only to the outcast Samaritans, He had come even to her.

Chapter 3
Carpenters Are for Mending

Mark 5:22-43

"Jesus Christ came into my prison cell last night

And every stone flashed like a ruby."

-Samuel Rutherford

We had been doctoring our little girl for days. But her fever kept growing higher. Now she no longer recognized us. Moans periodically escaped her throat as she thrashed around on her damp and steamy bed. We stood a helpless vigil by her side. Fear wrapped itself around our own throats while death seemed to stomp about the room shouting, "She'll not live, she's going to die."

Then her moans turned into a ghostly gasp that stood my husband to his feet. He hesitated for a moment, staring at her, then began heading for the door. I reached out and grabbed his arm. "Jairus, where are you going? You can't leave!" Gently but with great urgency, he took my hands in his and said, "We have been waiting for the Messiah our whole lives. If anyone ever seemed like He might be the One, it is that carpenter from Nazareth. And if He is the Messiah, then life and death are in His hands." He gently pressed my own hands as he looked into my eyes and gently said, "I'm going to search for him."

The door remained open behind him as he ran. Helplessly, I watched him go, not wanting to take my eyes from the hope that was in his steps. Yet what could have possessed him to leave me at a time like this? His judgment has surely gone amiss. A carpenter? A carpenter might repair our broken chair, but what good is a carpenter for the broken body of our precious daughter?

Then another moan captured my attention. "O God, don't let her die," I cried as I sat watching my daughter in disbelief. Incapable of relieving her sickness I sat helplessly by her bed. Wet cloths upon her head seemed so useless. Then a gasp escaped her parched and swollen lips and her fevered body stiffened. I reached out to hold her but with one more gasp, she slipped out of my reaching arms, falling back onto the damp sheets. And then she was still. Too still.... Only still. Only silence remained. A deadly silence.

I tentatively reached out again to touch her afraid of what I already knew. That we'd lost the fight and my daughter had lost her weakened grip on life. A wail came from deep within me growing in intensity with my agony. "No, no! God don't let this happen. This is too much. This can't be.... I can't...."

At my cry, Rivkeh[24] who had come to help nurse her along with two other women rushed to her side. After a moment or two of stark realization, without any hesitation, Rivkeh tenderly pulled the sheet over her unmoving body. At that, I turned away not able to bear the agony. The voices of the women who spoke to me faded away as my mind fought desperately for a place to hide. I turned toward the door where I had last seen my husband running in search of life-giving hands. "Too late," I moaned, "too late," and then called out in alarm as if he could hear me, "Jairus – where are you? Where are you? Come home. I need you."

Rivkeh attempted to calm my fright. "We'll send someone to find him," she said. "He'll be here soon." She smoothed my hair away from my face attempting to soothe my terrified state. How long I sat there with unseeing eyes, too stunned to cry, I do not know. The next thing I remember was Rivkeh trying to give me something to eat. Only the living eat, I thought and pushed it away with a hand almost too heavy to lift. What good would food be to me now? I too was now dead inside, dead like my daughter. So young, so sweet, she went to her death like a lamb to the slaughter. Pain filled my belly – no room for food – leaving almost no room even to breathe and too stunned even to grieve.

Someone moved me out of her room and sat me elsewhere, but I was only aware of being wrapped in a cocoon of my sorrow. There would be no hope ever again for tomorrow. Time came to a standstill and I sat

---

[24] *Rivkeh* is Hebrew for Rebecca.

numbed to anything but my loss and the terrible cost of my daughter.

Sometime later the smell of spices brought me to my senses and I became aware of voices in the bedroom. Rivkeh and the others were taking great care to begin to prepare her body for burial. "No. Not yet. Too soon," I managed to say. Rivkeh came to my side and putting her hand on my face she began to croon words of comfort in her attempts to ease my pain. Prepare her for burial? It was impossible to even think of my daughter in a tomb. I recoiled at the thought. No, daughters are for life! Daughters are for living. I sat rocking to the rhythm of my agony while activity went on around me.

Then suddenly, a light pierced my misery. A light that seemed almost too bright broke into the heaviness in the house as the heavy wooden door was pushed open. My husband ran to me, his faced flushed with excitement. "I have found Him," he cried. "The one they call the Son of David. The carpenter!" I looked into his expectant face. I tried to tell him that it was too late. But he was too excited to listen to my barely audible voice. "He has come. He will heal her and renew her life," Jairus said with excitement. I knew what he meant but the time for healing had gone by hours before.

Even so, I looked toward the door at the Man standing in the light. As He stepped into the room an immediate sense of safety and *shalom*[25] seemed to enter with Him and wrap itself around me. Confused by His effect on me,

---

[25] Peace

my eyes followed Him as He began to usher the neighbors out of the house. Why He acts as if this were His house, this carpenter. Who does He think He is?

I desperately wanted my husband's attention, but he was now leading the carpenter to the bedroom where our still daughter lay, now bathed and prepared according to ritual for the next stage of what is required for burial. Too weak and confused to do much more than watch, I slid again into my own distorted thoughts.

My poor husband, he was in such a hurry to get that carpenter to her. But he seems in no hurry, that carpenter. He seems so undisturbed. Has He no feelings inside? Did He not care that our daughter has died? Do neither of them even know it? Jairus hasn't even realized she's no longer with us. Oh, how I wish this Man would go away and leave us alone so my husband can know of our loss. How I need Jairus to share this tragedy with me.

Then I realized the Man was standing in front of me. Tenderly He put His hand on my elbow and helped me to my feet. Without any questions, I rose to His beckoning and found that I felt that safe feeling again. I tried to understand but I could say nothing. I could only lean my weight against the strength of Him to support me as He walked me into the room where she lay. I tried not to sway in my unsteadiness while my thoughts continued to bewilder me. I would have to go with this Man wherever He would lead me, my thoughts told me. Then fearfully I decided I must be losing my sanity.

At the sight of my daughter lying pale and motionless, I tried desperately to keep control of my emotions lest I really did depart from reality. I would have fainted had the carpenter not been supporting me. He sat me in a nearby chair. I could no longer make any sense of what was happening. He was talking to her. Why is He speaking to one who can never hear again? He's holding her hand as if to comfort her. There is no comfort. Not anymore. Yet I continued to listen to His words as He said to her, *"Talitha, Cumi"* – "*Little girl, arise,*" as if she were alive.

He's speaking to her as if He expects she can hear Him, I thought, confused. Am I crazy, or is He? And He looks at her as if she were His own daughter, this carpenter from Nazareth. I was afraid to hope, yet I watched Him, captivated by something in Him I could not comprehend. What was it that He had said? Arise? I looked at her limp body on the bed.

But what was this sound I just heard? It could not be coming from her! No, I will not allow myself to imagine a fantasy. I must hold onto reality. I must accept the truth, I told myself. Then the sound, it came again, and then…she moved! How could this be? My thoughts were so hazy, surely it was I who must be going crazy.

Then the carpenter lovingly laid His hand on her forehead. When He took it away, there was color in her cheeks such as we had not seen for many weeks. A brief moment later, to my greatest surprise, she opened her eyes! Then her eyes found mine and as if everything was as it had always been, she smiled.

I watched as Jairus fell upon the bed clutching her to his chest, weeping with joy. Still terrified that this was but the imagination of an insane person – me, I was too paralyzed to react. Until, that is, the carpenter came and knelt before me and said, "Your little girl is alive." I looked into His face trying to grasp what had just happened. "Go hold her. Your daughter has been given back to you."

Slowly, with His help, I stood and walked to where my husband and daughter were wrapped in each other's embrace. I reached out for her. "*Ima*, oh *Ima*!" she cried as I buried my face now wet with tears into her neck. She no longer smelled like someone who was sick. Now she smelled of new life, like the baby she once was. I could not hold her close enough.

A short time later, I handed my little girl to her father and walked to where the Carpenter was standing. He was smiling while watching us from the corner of the room with the few friends of His who had come with Him. I stood before Him looking at Him with awe. His eyes spoke of such compassion, yet I could think of nothing to say. "Thank you" would never have been enough. Somehow, I knew that He understood what was in my heart and what I wished I could tell Him. He reached out and put His hand on my arm. I covered His hand with mine, looking deeply and gratefully into His eyes. Again, I had that great sense of *shalom*, but now I knew why. "*How about giving her something to eat?*" He whispered. I nodded, my heart overflowing with joy. I went to hold her once again before going to make her some food.

The carpenter and his friends stayed with us for a meal. I must admit I was just a bit embarrassed when the one they called Shimon Kefa[26] had reached for a chair to

---

[26] *Shimon Kefa* in Hebrew is Simon Peter in English.

pull it up to our table, and it turned out to be the chair with the broken rung, which would not have been able to hold the size of him. We offered him another chair. As we ate, we all laughed and enjoyed each other, singing songs of thanksgiving to the Lord together, our daughter being the star of the party.

Later that evening, Jairus and I were talking about our miracle that day long after our little girl was tucked away into a clean and fresh bed for the night and I was cleaning up from the dinner. "Imagine," I said, "I had thought, of what help could a carpenter be? But then Yeshua came and everything changed." I moved the extra chairs back against the wall and that's when I saw it. "Jairus, look at this. Another miracle." We both laughed as we saw that the broken rung of the chair was now straight and as good as new.

Chapter 4
Paralyzed No More

Matthew 9:1-9; Mark 2:1-12

*"Something in (His) eyes, more persuasive than any
I ever saw… that sort of nameless excellence"*
-Lawrence Sterne (1762)

I had forgotten what it was like to walk, to be able to care for myself and go where I wanted, to run through the village and into the meadow where the sight of softly swaying stalks of sun-drenched grains fill my heart with delight. I'd forgotten even what it was like to walk across the cool shuttered rooms to the kitchen to join with my brothers and any others who were there, eating eye to eye.

They brought me my food upon a tray and set me where I would not be in the way. They carried me. My brothers had to carry me! Them and sometimes my friend Yossi[27] too who still remembers when we played tag among the trees and scooped tadpoles from the trickling

---

[27] *Yossi*, a short name for Yosef (Joseph).

stream and told each other stories until the fires turned to glowing embers.

But everything was different today. They were giving me no choice, ignoring my voice of dissent. I had no say. Today, they say, we are going to see the Healer, that Yeshua, the one from Nazareth. Miracles, they tell me and their voices ring with excited intentions to make me one of them. "I don't want to go," I tell them. But they were so sure of what they intend and since I could not get off my bed I was borne along in dread to the destination they had determined for me.

When we arrived, crowds of people barricaded the door leaving no expectations of me being carried in. Though I begged to go home I knew there was no hope. They would win over my protests and my pleading would fall upon their deaf ears. Then I heard cheers from within the house: "He hears! He hears!" as someone was freed from a lifetime of deafness by this Yeshua, this healer from Nazareth.

Always somebody else, I thought. I swallowed the familiar sense of failure and being left out that had been my daily bread ever since That Day. There is no way, not anymore, I told myself. I'll have to pay and live out my days upon this litter, causing others to bear this bitter task of carrying me as the burden they are destined to bear.

I was suddenly shaken from my self-absorbing reverie and was jostled on my bed as I was lifted high above their heads. My brothers, who with uplifted arms pulled me with ropes they found somewhere, up into the air, past the windows and clearing the cross beams to the roof above where Ya'acov was waiting. I settled with a thud. It made me wonder if being this high made me any closer to God.

I marveled that they'd done it, and that they'd cared for me this much, that each would play a part to bring me here. They had such hope, I knew, but the thought of further failure brought the fear of disappointing them again and brought panic to my already pounding heart. "Now what?" I asked them tentatively, afraid of what they intended next, concerned they would ask something of me I could not give them. But they knew what I could not do. They knew all too well without my having to tell them.

Still, my thoughts were racing through my head. What next, I wondered with a dread. Then suddenly dirt was flying everywhere and I was tasting dust and all I could do was watch as they dug a hole in the roof after lifting off the thatch. "Hey! What's going on up there?" shouted someone from below. Oh how I just wanted it all to end. But there surely was no way to make them stop. If only I could just hop off this bed and fly away. But it was clear I'd have to stay and see this through, whatever my brothers and Yossi were determined to do.

And then again, with the ropes they'd found, they lowered me down upon my bed to just in front of the Man who stood and said something about how much faith my brothers had to be so determined that they'd bring the lad to Him through a hole in the roof. He seemed not annoyed but delighted, even touched by this act of what He called courageous faith. His words about faith stirred something inside me. All of a sudden I knew that I could face whatever would happen. Somehow, I sensed there would be no disgrace, the very thing I feared the most.

This Man bent down to talk with me at my level and His eyes... His eyes – what color were they? I cannot recall, for all colors seemed to be at home in Him, as if in His eyes – in those eyes – it was as if He Himself was also everyone else. And even me. I can't explain what I seemed to see.

But then, He looked into my own eyes as if He saw into the core of me and He said to me, "*Son, your sins are forgiven.*" At this, the crowd grew quiet. Deafeningly silent. But I was not concerned with them. I could only try and grasp what He just said. Forgiven? Again and again, the words repeated in my head. Even so, my thoughts came quickly and suddenly I was back on That Day when my poor choice had sent me hurling down an emotional ravine that had left me reeling and so devastated, I could hardly move.

How could I have allowed it? I was powerless against it. And afterward, I had lain there in my misery in darkened silence for so long that when I tried to move I couldn't. And ever since, even the thought, even a flicker of remembrance of That Day would bring me such dismay that it kept me paralyzed inside, like part of me had died, and the rest of me was in mourning, and unable to rise.

Forgiven, He said. He's forgiven me of my sin? How can He do that? He's just another man. But I looked again into His eyes - His eyes! - and saw reflected there myself as if my sin was absorbed into His very being. And then, I knew that it was true. I knew! I was forgiven, as if my sin had never been. That Day, I knew, no longer had control over me and I was free to live again!

While I was still trying to process this and have it all make sense to me, a discussion was going on between some men, each wrapped in a large *tallit*.[28] Looking right at them, Yeshua said, sternly this time, "*So you will know that the Son of Man can forgive the sins of men …*" Then He turned and looked at me again and said, "*Son, take up your bed a walk.*" I had been so overwhelmed and awed that my guilt had fled that I had forgotten I was still upon my bed. I looked inside myself for the usual dread and for the hopelessness, but they were gone.

Carefully I bent my knees and slowly stood upon my legs which no longer felt like useless pegs. Straightening up inch by inch, I felt the strength grow in my body. I reached for His arm to steady me but He had already reached for me, to be there as I needed Him, until I stood erect. The crowd cheered, at least most of them, though a few in the throng scowled as if He'd done something wrong. But I didn't listen for long. This was so right. This was so good. And from where I now stood I lifted my arms to my brothers and Yossi who peered down through the hole in the roof above where they'd watched from that height and who now were cheering with all of their might.

With a love I'd never known before I gave praise to *Adonai* and great thanks to Yeshua. "*Pick up your bed and go home,*" He said. I gathered my litter under my arm and climbed over the people in the room who made a way

---

[28] Prayer shawl

for me to walk through the crowd as they cheered me on. Then I ran – yes, I ran – outside to Yossi and my brothers who met me there with great joy and huge hugs as they lifted me off of the ground while spinning me around. Then they watched me walk and then jump and then leap in the sunshine. What I had wanted for so long I now could do since my brother and Yossi brought me to Yeshua. I didn't know how to thank them, but from the joy on their faces, I didn't think I had to. They knew how grateful I was. Finally, I realized, I could decide! And with that realization, I said, "Come on. Let's go home," as I started to walk into my future where my life was waiting for me to begin again.

Chapter 5

Zaccheus' Short Story

Luke 19:1-10

"We trust not because God exists,
but because this God exists!"

-C.S. Lewis

All I can tell you is that all of my life my own personal strife was that I was short. It was hard to have no one take you seriously, always on the fringe of the crowd, as if I wasn't allowed to be a part of what everyone else was. So, I found a way to overcome the rejection and became a businessman of sorts, if you call being a chief tax collector a business. I also collected some beautiful things, seeking the value in the things that I owned. As I saw it, both kinds of collection gave me some recognition despite my condition of being so short.

But I have to say on that day when Yeshua came to town everything changed. I had heard about Him, of course, everyone had, of how He'd freed a lad of a malformed leg and brought a little girl back from the dead. But what amazed me most from the stories I was hearing, as if all that wasn't enough, was the hope He was bringing of God's Kingdom to us. Not later... in the future... one day... someday. But with us. Now. Here. In our day. Messiah? He must be. Who else could He be?

A fleeting thought went through my mind - What if I could have Him dine at my house tonight? What a privilege that would be. Ah, but how could that be? There's such a crowd. He isn't likely to even notice me. Still, when He came I tried to see Him. And as I pushed through the crowd I called to Him out loud, "Yeshua... can You see me?" Then fearing I'd again be left out I repeated with more cadence this time than a shout. "Yeshua, can...You... see... me?" But alas, I knew He wouldn't. Because He couldn't. I was just too short.

Yet more than anything, even if He couldn't see me, I wanted to see *Him*. So, I shimmied up a tree just as He came near. I could hear His wonderful hope-filling voice speaking to others. One was a mother with a sick child. Then another, and another. And then, Yeshua came, just under my tree and He looked up - as if He was looking to see...me! To my greatest surprise as I looked down at Him - He looked right into my eyes. And called me by my name. How did He know it? And then He said, *"Zaccheus, I will have supper at your house tonight."* Just as if I had invited Him... as if He had heard my earlier wish.

I was so dumbfounded I lost my grip and with a swish I fell out of the tree. He laughed as He caught my arm so I suffered no harm. Then without any hesitation I told Him the location of my home and then I went off to prepare. And soon enough He was there - in my home!

Eating dinner with me! And some friends I'd invited to join us. Me and Messiah – Oh how Joyous!!

Well, that wasn't all that happened that day. He did come for supper as if I was part of the upper crust of our town. Not that it mattered to Him. Not at all. He welcomes us all equally, I found out. Rich or poor, short or tall. It really doesn't matter if you're tall or you're small because *Adonai* has no favorites. He loves us all.

That day for me marked a new start. There was such a change in my heart. For the first time in my life, I felt deep inside as if I was actually tall! Even so, most important of all, I came to know that our value in life has nothing really to do with our size or even how much that we own or how important we are. It's about being aware of God's attention and care. And how we are each seen in His eyes as being His own. And that has made all the difference to me ever since Yeshua came to dine at my home.

Chapter 6
The Agony of Betrayal

Matthew 26:73-75; John 21:1-11

"Mercy has converted more souls than zeal, or eloquence, or learning, or all of them together."

-Soren Kierkegaard

Hopelessness hissed at the hiding disciples huddled together in the upper room. Punctuated by periods of silence, they shared their fears, their questions, and their sorrows. Except for Peter[29] who for once was silent.

How could this happen, they asked each other, questions ricocheting between them? How could one so powerful become so weak? Yeshua's words had confounded even the most articulate *P'rushim*[30] before.

---

[29] Although Peter's real Hebrew name was *Shimon,* and though Yeshua nicknamed him *Kefa* which is a small rock, I have chosen to keep his name as Peter in this story to maintain the familiarity most readers have with him as Peter.

[30] Pharisees in Hebrew

Why could He not speak in His own defense? They'd never defeated Him earlier. Why now? What happened? What changed? And what was to become of them? How are they to put their lives together again? What were they to do without Him? They couldn't go back to what life was before. They were no longer the men they once were.

What if the ones who were to blame for Yeshua's death now wanted to find His followers? What would the leaders do to them after what they had done to Him? Fear rippled through the room. While they shared their confusion, another dialog was going as Peter, crouched in a corner, was immersed in shame, berated himself over and over again.

He told me. He warned me. He told me I'd deny Him. And I did it. He was right. I'm nothing more than a coward. Oh, I had big dreams. I'd lay down my life for Him. "Anything, Lord," I told Him. I expected He'd rise to the grandeur of His calling and show them all who He really was, that He was really the Messiah and surely one day soon He'd be like David and would reign as King. Oh, I thought I could see everything so clearly. I was so sure that I, above the others, could see all the omens. Soon it would be all over for the Romans.

Sure, I was brave enough when I thought He was victorious, when I believed it would all be glorious. Then I'd sing, oh how I'd sing His praises. But where was I for the Man I called my friend when He was in need and I turned out to reject Him the way He said I would? How could I abandon Him like that? And even come so low as to deny any connection with Him? "I don't even know Him,'" I told them and I betrayed the only Man I've ever known to be righteous. All my boasting was nothing but empty words, a net with great holes.

Was I following Him because of who He was...or because of who I thought I would become, because of what I expected I would eventually get out of it? I would be famous alongside of Him, I thought. But all my boasting and intentions amounted to nothing.

A groan of pain escaped from Peter's throat adding to his shame as he threw a quick glance around the room to see if anyone heard him or noticed him muttering to himself... or to see if anyone knew how unworthy he now was to even still be counted among them.

But they all seemed too absorbed in their own anguish to notice. Peter turned back to his thoughts. *If only I could tell Him how sorry I am. If only....* But Peter knew it was hopeless. *He's gone. He's dead. It's over. All over.... And such an unthinkable tragic end.* At that thought, he wrapped his arms more tightly around himself and turned his face even further into the darkened corner.

And then, a furious knocking attacked the door causing them all to freeze with terror. The voice of Miryam from Magdala[31] shouted, "Open the door. I've seen Him. I've seen the Lord." Looking at each other with confused glances, one of them quickly opened the door

---

[31] Every N.T. Mary had the Hebrew name of Miryam. This Miryam's last name wasn't Magdalene as most translations say. She was Miryam from the town of Magdala, a fishing village in the Galilee.

lest the noise of her voice attract attention. Flushed and excited she repeated her declaration, "He's alive. I tell you, He's alive."

Their response was not what she anticipated. She hadn't imagined she'd be rejected. "Miryam, sit down. You've been through too much," the men said as one by one they tried to calm her, including John with a reassuring touch. "He's dead. Gone, Miryam. It's over. Dead is dead!" But Miryam only shook her head and went on to tell them all over again.

As Peter listened from the darkened corner his heart began to throb within him. *Could it be? He raised others from the dead. Is it possible that He....?* Not finishing the sentence in his own mind, he stood to his feet, his eyes meeting John's and immediately in silent agreement they both made for the door and started to run. They got to Joseph's tomb where Yeshua had been laid after wrapping His body with spice-infused burial cloths just three days ago. Gasping for breath after running the whole way John peered through the opening but it was Peter who entered. Then he stood, stunned and silent, staring at the place where Yeshua's body should have been.

But it wasn't there. The tomb was empty! Only the grave cloths remained with the head cloth nearby. What did this mean? Could it be true? Was He really alive as Miryam had said?

They couldn't begin to know where to find Him. There was nothing to do but go back to where the rest of the men were and wait. If He was alive surely He would come to them. Once again in the upper room they all went over and over the things He had said, trying to make sense out of it all, when all at once in a moment's time... there He was, as if it was natural for Him to arrive this way.

One moment He wasn't there and the next He was, right before their eyes. He didn't knock on the bolted door or walk into the room. He was just suddenly there among them! He greeted them as He always had with His usual *Shalom Alechem.*[32] All they could do is stare at Him, speechless at first as they were all in shock. But the silence was quickly replaced with utterances of joy even though they had trouble believing He was really standing in front of them, very much alive!

Peter, overwhelmed at seeing Him, wanted to wrap his arms around Him in a giant hug, or throw himself at His feet, or look into His eyes – anything to somehow tell Him how unspeakably sorry he was that he had failed Him. But his shame kept him on the outskirts of the group though he watched every move Yeshua made and tried to draw into himself every expression on His face and every word that He said. Like one who loves but is afraid to approach the loved one for fear of being rejected, Peter listened from a distance.

His agony increased as he looked on, horrified by the ugly scars as Yeshua reached out His nail-pierced hands to show them His wounds. Overwhelmed with sorrow Peter told himself, *I'm the one that deserves those wounds, not Him.* He tried to focus on His words as Yeshua gently rebuked them for their unbelief. But then, in the same voice with which He'd sent them out not so

---

[32] *Shalom Alechem* means peace be unto you. It is still the way many Jewish people and Israeli's greet one another.

very long ago, telling them to *"heal the sick, raise the dead, and cast out demons,"* He was telling them now to go again. This time, He said to wait for power from on high and then go to declare the Kingdom to all the world, immersing people in the waters of *Mikveh*[33] in His name. Not sure exactly what He meant, they nevertheless waited faithfully, anticipating *Shavuot*.[34]

How far were they to go? To all the world, He said. They were to make others into their own *talmidim*,[35] just as they had been His *talmidim*. At that, guilt rose up within Peter again at his failure to be a faithful disciple. *However, could I be one who could fulfill what He's saying? He's telling us to be fishers of men, but I've disqualified myself from serving Him by my betrayal, the very thing I thought I'd never do.*

Despite his joy at seeing Yeshua alive - more alive than He'd ever seen Him, or anyone for that matter! – Peter knew his own weakness of character would keep him from ever being able to join the others in fulfilling Yeshua's new commandment of the work they were to do for Him. Then, as Peter's sorrow seemed unbearable, just as suddenly as He came, Yeshua was gone again.

---

[33] *Mikveh* is baptism in Hebrew, which literally means immersion – a practice that had been going on in Israel since Moses for religious purification.

[34] Shavuot is also known as Pentecost. See Acts 3.

[35] *Talmidim* (pronounced tahl-mih-DEEM) means disciples. It was common for rabbis to have their own *talmidim*. But Yeshua's disciples were to become born again and Spirit-filled people of God.

Pandemonium broke out among the men as they laughed and hugged each other and told each other over and over what He had said. Peter pretended to be excited, but it was only that, a pretense. He was absolutely miserable. He was still drowning in the guilt of his betrayal. Yet no one seemed to notice. At least not then.

Days went by. Not knowing what else to do, Peter remained with them. The disciples were awed and excited. They chattered noisily over and over about what they would be doing, how they would do it and where they would go, while trying to imagine what it all meant. They spent hours remembering Scriptures they now saw all pointed to Yeshua.

Peter pretended to be enthusiastic with them and they pretended not to notice his sadness. John, however, acutely aware of his friend's despair kept one eye on Peter as they made their plans. Unable to endure their joy one moment longer Peter abruptly announced, "I'm going fishing."[36] "I'll go with you," John quickly said with feigned enthusiasm, unwilling to allow Peter to go off by himself in his present state of mind, knowing what had taken place when Peter denied knowing the Lord. The others decided it would do them good to get out on the sea again after being in the city for so long. So together they made their way to the Galilee and their boats.

It was almost dawn. They had caught not one fish between them. Their all-night futile efforts for a

---

[36] This entire part of Peter's story is found in John 21.

catch matched Peter's sense of his own empty self-worth. Sitting in the boat, bobbing with the gentle waves slapping up against it, nets in the water, the rocking motion kept cadence with Peter's own morose thoughts.

If only…if only I could see Him…if I could just see Him…all by myself… Just us. If only…if only I could tell Him…how truly sorry I am… I hurt Him… I know that… When He needed a friend…I betrayed Him… He knew it…Before it happened, He knew it… The look that He gave me…that night in the courtyard…I'll never forget it… I'll never escape it…oh, wretched man that I am… Will I never be free…of this agony?

Then a voice called from the shore interrupting his excruciating reverie. Someone was addressing the fish they had not caught as if he knew they'd caught none. The man called out to them, *"Throw your nets over the right side of the boat and you'll find a catch!"*

Something about the voice as it called from the shore was familiar. At the very second that he remembered hearing similar words from Yeshua years ago, at the beginning, John cried out, "It is the Lord!" Peter's eyes scanned the shore for the lone figure standing on the beach by a fire. Grabbing his tunic, he yanked it over his head as he threw himself into the water swimming as hard as he could for shore. He had to get alone with the Lord and this was his one chance. Lungs burning and muscles near failure he swam the distance until he reached the shallow water.

Staggering across the pebble-strewn shore[37] he threw himself at the feet of Yeshua. He lay there for a few moments not knowing which was greater, the pain in his lungs or the anguish in his heart. Opening his eyes, his gaze fell upon the puncture wounds in Yeshua's ankles.[38] They matched the ones in His wrists and in His side which He had shown to Thomas. Too horrified and overwhelmed to speak, Peter lay there trying to calm his racing heart.

Yeshua stood above him, quietly waiting for Peter to process what he was seeing. Then He gently laid His hand upon Peter's heaving shoulder. At the touch of His hand, there erupted from the deepest part of Peter's soul, King David's own words of anguished repentance: "*Choneni, Elohim. Kerov rachamecha mechey feshai.* Be gracious to me, O Lord. According to the multitude of Your mercies, blot out my transgressions."[39]

And with the release of those words, Peter could no longer hold back the tormenting emotions which gripped him as deep wracking sobs overcame him. After several moments, when his anguish was spent, Yeshua raised him up to his knees. Looking full into Peter's swollen eyes, His hands upon Peter's shoulders, Yeshua said, "I love you, Simon. You are entirely forgiven."

---

[37] The shores of the Sea of Galilee are of pebbles rather than sand. It is not really a sea but a giant lake.

[38] The nails were likely in Yeshua's wrists and ankles for Roman efficiency purposes, though the words used are hands and feet.

[39] Psalm 51:1

Peter searched the Beloved Face before him and found in Yeshua's eyes a sense of being *echad*,[40] of being one in spirit with Him in a way that he hadn't known before, even through all the years they had spent together. It came to Peter as a sudden flash of revelation that Yeshua was now fully alive though He had in fact been dead, and that when He had died He had taken sin with Him! Even his own sin! And in those few seconds of realization, just like that, all of Peter's guilt left him! In that isolated moment it seemed to Peter as if no one else existed and no one else mattered other than Yeshua.

A peace such as he'd never known began to seep through Peter's entire being. He looked deeply and gratefully into the eyes of His Lord who offered Peter an understanding expression as if He knew all Peter had gone through, including here on the lake shore and what Peter had just fully grasped of the meaning of His resurrection. With a smile Peter would never forget, Yeshua said to him, "Now go help the others bring in the catch." At His word, Peter ran toward the others to join them in the work they all had to do.

---

[40] *Echad* is a oneness in nature, not in number. This would be the kind of oneness Yeshua wants for us that He prayed for when He asked His Father that "they may all be one, just as we are one" (John 17: 21-22).

Chapter 7
No Longer Just My Brother

James 1:1 & 2

"I believe in [Yeshua] as I believe that the sun has risen, Not only because I see it, but because by [Him] I see everything else"
-C.S. Lewis [paraphrased]

"Ya'acov, a servant of Yehova[41] *and of Adonai Yeshua HaMashiach. To the twelve tribes which are scattered abroad, Shalom."*[42]

I got that far as I sat at my writing table. With the fresh quill tip poised between my fingers, I pensively thought of what it was that I wanted to say to my fellow Jews who were so far from Jerusalem, even dispersed a far distance away. As a leader now among the believers in Yeshua, I

---

[41] This is the name of God, often written with only the consonants as YHVH, which is used in the original Old Testament text approximately 7,000 times. Israeli believers today often use His name this way. As Yeshua is referred to as Lord, which would be *Adonai*, I have used *Yehova* to mean God the Father.

[42] This is how the first words written in James 1:1 would have read to the Hebrews receiving his letter: *Ha* (the) *Mashiach* (Messiah).

felt a great burden to strengthen those who were suffering persecution because of their belief in Him.

Two of my own disciples were there in the room with me waiting to make the journey to take the letter to those I was writing to. "They are up against a great challenge to their faith," I said to them, sharing my reason for the importance of this letter getting to its destination. "I know what that is like," I added, "when faced with confusion as to the conflicts that arise around believing in Yeshua."

"Tell us about your own experiences, Ya'acov," one of the disciples asked. "Yes, tell us," the other one echoed. As I pondered what to say next, even where to begin, my mind drifted back past my own challenges of faith to the childhood we had shared. And so, I began my story of what it was like to be Yeshua's brother.

Growing up, our parents taught us the ways of *Yehova* as if they had a personal investment in us seeing the significance of them. I remember them stressing the importance of remaining faithful to His Word, no matter the challenges. I didn't see the significance of our parents' words then as I do now. We learned story after story of the challenges to the faith of Israel through the centuries. It was especially *Ima*, after *Abba* was gone, who emphasized to us children the faithfulness of those who trusted in *Yehovah* and His promises, even in times when the love of most in Israel had grown cold toward Him.

She talked to us of the prophets and their ability to hear what *Yehova* was saying to His people, words that should always be taken seriously even though years had passed since the prophets uttered those words. And she told us of the prophesies of the coming Messiah, of who He would be, and how He would be identified as *"Adonai with us"*[43] and how He would set Israel free from sin and oppression. Oh, how we longed to be free of the oppression of Rome that rested so heavily upon all of Israel.

I remember now how *Ima's* eyes would wander over to Yeshua at times, but He never responded any differently than any of us did, except, that Yeshua always seemed to have some insights that neither me nor our brothers or sisters ever seemed to have. On occasion, I felt somewhat jealous of the way Yeshua always had the right answer to questions any of us were asking or a solution to every problem, But He was so loveable that it was hard to stay annoyed with Him for very long. He was just...well, good.

Our favorite stories were of the miracles, and the wonderful ways that *Yehova* proved Himself to be the Redeemer of Israel, time and time again. *Ima's* voice had emphasizing how God's words always proved to be true. Even when one of the prophets was rejected, she told us, and his message was disregarded by our people, though the prophets had suffered greatly, *Yehova* had used them to remind the people of His ways and in time Israel would return to Him. It was her expectation that soon, in our day, all Israel would once again turn to *Yehovah.*

---

[43] The phrase *"Adonai* with us" is the name *Emanu-El* in Hebrew.

When we were younger, many times my brothers, Yeshua, Y'hudah, Yosef, and Shimon[44] and I would retell the Bible stories to one another. We'd act them out with toy men we carved from the remnants of *Abba's* wood scraps. Yeshua and I, as the two oldest, were especially close. He was the easiest to get along with of all my brothers. And even as we grew up, Yeshua was liked by everyone.

After my brothers and sisters and I began to marry, though Yeshua seemed genuinely happy for us all, He never seemed to have much interest in finding a wife for Himself, even though there were many women who seemed to take enough of a liking to Him. Still, He never responded to their flirting or affections. In fact, He never treated anyone more special than anyone else.

But then something happened to Him sometime around His thirtieth birthday. One day Yeshua just disappeared. We almost always knew where He was because He carried much of the responsibility of our carpentry business, especially since we lost our father, though it had been a number of years now. Oh yes, He would wander off sometimes, usually early in the morning to pray, but He was always back in time to open the shop or begin our work.

But then, one day, off He went, and we had no idea where. Although *Ima* seemed especially quiet about it,

---

[44] See Matthew 13:55. Their Hebrew names have gone through several translations. Those translations are loosely shown here as: Yacov to Jacob to James; Yehuda to Judah to Jude; Shimon to Simon; and Yosef (or Yossi) to Joseph.

only saying, "He'll be back when He's ready to be back," she encouraged us to keep the family business going without Him. It seemed forever that He was gone.

One day, about a month later, He was back. But He was different. Thinner for one thing, and He had a bit of a wild look about Him, as if something had changed Him, almost as if He had some purpose come upon Him but He wasn't explaining it to us. He had come home to us, but He didn't even give any explanation to us as to where He had been, other than some discussion about meeting that *Yohanan ha matbil*[45], that so-called prophet who was immersing people in the Jordan River as they supposedly repented of their sins. We had no idea what to make of it all.

On the *Shabbat*[46] after He returned, our family was in our village synagogue as usual. Though He had been sitting with the family, at one point He stood up and went to the *bima*[47] where the Torah scroll was opened to the day's reading. This in itself was not unusual for He was already one of the men at His age of thirty who was permitted to read from it. But when He began to unravel the scroll to another place, other than the reading for that week, it caught everyone's attention as this was out of the order and highly irregular.[48]

---

[45] John the Immerser, or baptizer.

[46] Sabbath

[47] A *bima* (bee-mah) is a platform or podium on which the Torah scroll was placed for reading.

[48] The Torah readings are always read on designated weeks during the year so that the readings always ended on *Sukkot* each year.

Then He began to read, His voice projecting while reading more slowly than was generally used when reading from Torah so that everyone could grasp what He was saying:

> *"The Spirit of Adonai is upon me because He has anointed me to preach the Gospel to the poor. He has sent me to proclaim release to the captives, and recovery of sight to the blind, to set free those who are oppressed, to proclaim the favorable year of Adonai."*[49]

Then He rerolled the scroll back to where it had been and gave it back to the attendant and sat down. The eyes of all in the synagogue were fixed on Him, including us. Then He said, *"Today, this Scripture is fulfilled in your hearing."* I could feel my heart beating with nervousness at the irregularity of it all. What was He doing? More importantly, what was He saying? And what were we to make of this? How embarrassing it was that the whole synagogue, people we had known our whole lives, had no idea how to deal with the way He was acting, or what He was implying.

He had read the words *"The Spirit of Adonai is upon me"* and looked around at everyone as if to make the point that He was the "me" in the text. He surely wasn't acting or talking like the Yeshua He had been as long as everyone had known Him. That even included His family!

If that wasn't enough, noticing that everyone was looking at Him and the service had not moved on, He

---

[49] Isaiah 61:1; Luke 4:18.

added some other things, going on to say, as if all this wasn't enough, something about the stories of the miracles they may have heard about Him that they now would like to see Him do here in His own hometown. And as if He was speaking intentionally to antagonize them, which seemed entirely out of character for my brother, He began to say things about how Elisha the prophet said some things to Israel but no one but a hated Syrian paid any attention and the Syrian was healed as a result.

Well, before we could get Him out of there, the entire synagogue, people who had always loved Him, suddenly were filled with rage at the things He was saying. Like one person, they rose up together as if someone was orchestrating the whole thing, and we were unable to do anything to stop them, though I certainly tried. Being swept along with the crowd, I soon realized they intended to push Him toward the end of town and throw Him off the cliff. I was terrified that it might actually happen but then He turned and just began to walk back through the crowd as if they had no power over Him. And just like that, He walked right out of town without coming back to our home or with any attempt to explain to us what just happened. He just left us standing there, humiliated, confused, and with no sense of when He would come home or what to expect next.

Ima hadn't gone with the crowd, of course. We didn't know what happened to her, but we found her at home, making dinner as usual. As much as we talked to her of how we as His family needed to rescue Him from whatever this was, at least at this point, she just remained rather silent about it, more like pensive, or thoughtful. What was she thinking? I asked her, but she said nothing that gave me or my brothers and sisters any sense that she knew any more than we did, though she was unusually quiet and seemed preoccupied, and on occasion, worried.

But still, she said nothing to any of us. Even our sisters who were very close to her could not find out what she was thinking about Yeshua's strange behavior. I determined that the next time He came home, He and I were going to have a serious talk about whatever was going on in His life. My concerns for Him were preoccupying me as well, but since His leaving left me with the responsibility of running the carpentry shop along with Yosef without His help, it kept me very busy as the business was doing well.

When people came through town, or our neighbors visited elsewhere, it seems they came back with stories about Yeshua. I never did get to have my intended talk with Him as He didn't come home very often now and on the few occasions when He did, He and *Ima* seemed to have some conversations that we were excluded from. And though He always seemed glad to be with us and still talked with us as He so often had about the ways of *Adonai* in the *Tenakh,*[50] He alluded to none of the reports we were hearing about Him, nor would He talk to us about them. He just acted as if none of it existed. It all seemed rather mysterious. In some ways, He was Yeshua

---

[50] *Tenakh* is the entire Hebrew Scriptures, also called the Old (or Older) Testament, the only Bible the people in the New Testament had.

just as He always was, but in other ways, even if we tried to ask Him about them, we knew there were things He wasn't telling us. What could they be?

The stories continued to filter through the gossip that went on about Him, though very few people talked directly to us as His family about them. Mostly they avoided us. When it seemed that people were huddled together telling stories they heard, as soon as they realized one of us from His family were approaching, their circle would break up and they would disperse, just nodding hello to us. The husband of one of our sisters made it very clear that he would not have her or their children anywhere near "that madman" when He came home.

My own children had always adored Uncle Yeshua and He had greatly enjoyed them from the time they were quite little. He had always loved children. And so, when we heard stories of Him and children when someone would actually tell it to one of us, they seemed in line with the Yeshua we knew. But the rest caused us great worry.

From what we could glean from the reports we were hearing, He was being called a rabbi by a great many people who gathered to hear what He was teaching them. But we also heard that He had developed a friendship with a tax collector that had joined His followers. Since when did tax collectors follow anyone even remotely the likes of a rabbi? And what was He thinking, hanging out with sinners at all?

Well, I knew how He could make the stories in the *Tenakh* come alive. So, I understood people's fascination with His story-telling. But from what we also heard, though many people sought Him out, now the *Tzadukim* and *P'rushim*[51] had become angry with Him. How godly could that be? The stories continued to filter down to us. It was so embarrassing to have people outside the family know more than we did, as often merchants coming through our town would tell us the stories, having no idea we were His family.

Finally, Yehuda and Yosef and I decided we'd had enough of this. That was when we convinced *Ima* that we just had to put an end to what was going on. *Ima* had finally shared with us some idea that she had that He might be the *Mashiach*.[52] Now we had her to worry about too. Add to this that we heard that some people were saying, "He has an unclean spirit. If He was the *Mashiach* He certainly wouldn't alienate the *Tzadokim* and *P'rushim*. Surely they would know if that's who Yeshua

---

[51] Pharisees: *P'rushim* (p'roo-SHEEM) in Hebrew, were men who were basically bible commentators and 'lawyers' who put their writings into what became rabbinic law. They added a great deal to the written *Torah* which were the very 'laws' Yeshua spoke against. Their zeal was for keeping those 'laws' they had added which became a kind of 'religion' of its own. However, they did believe in life after death and the moves of the Spirit. Many of them became believers in Yeshua.

Sadducees: *Tzadokim* (Tsah-doe-KEEM) are the high priestly descendants of Aaron who served in the temple but who for the most part were not righteous. Their focus was largely on the *Torah* exclusively – no prophets - and they didn't believe in life after death or the Holy Spirit, so they apparently had no qualms or fears about the eternal consequences of putting Yeshua to death. It was they who were most responsible for murdering Yeshua.

[52] Messiah.

was." Why couldn't *Ima* see that? This was all becoming too much! Something had to be done.

Even if some of this was remotely true, He shouldn't be alienating the very men who should have welcomed Him and supported Him. Whether *Ima* agreed with us or she decided to go along with our plan to rescue Him so she would be there for Him, the day came when we as His family went off to find Him.

It wasn't hard to locate Him, even though He was traipsing all around the country with a bunch of fishermen and, of all things, that tax collector. We often heard people saying various things about Him when we asked if anyone knew where He was. Many had only praise for Him, but others said things like: "What man of *Adonai* would spend time with sinful people? He even eats with them, and He spends no time with the priests in the temple."

Finally, we located a house where He was teaching. The house overflowed with people, many inside the house and a number crowding around the door and windows to hear what He was saying. We even saw a few men on the top of the house who seemed to be trying to make a hole in the roof with what looked like the intent to lower some man on a stretcher through it to get him near Yeshua. Madness, all of it.

As there was no way to get through the crowd to Him, we managed to get a message to Him that we were there for Him. Surely, we expected, He would come outside to us, and even be glad to see us. Our plan was to then take Him home with us. But I was about to learn that where my brother was concerned, my expectations of Him were no longer the Yeshua I grew up with. A message finally came back to us. Not Him, but a message *from* Him! The man with the message seemed at first embarrassed but then, he lifted his head as if he'd made a decision to tell us and said, "Yeshua told me to tell you that His mother and His brothers and sisters are those who do the will of God." [53]

Incredulous! I was dumbfounded at first but then, quickly recovering, I said to the man who gave us the message, "Did you tell him that His family was here for Him?" He opened his hands, palms up and said, "That's all I can tell you. He already knows and that's what He said to tell you." I was furious. I had never been so humiliated in my life. What kind of rejection was this? And what of my poor mother? She looked as if she had been slapped. At first, none of us moved, but then one of my sisters who had come along with us led *Ima* away from the crowd and just held her. Or was *Ima* holding her? I couldn't tell. My brothers were as angry as I was. I thought Y'hudah was going to punch someone, he was so angry.

"Who does He think He is?" Y'hudah shouted as we moved out of the crowd in the other direction from those who were still trying to hear what Yeshua was saying. "I'd like to remind Him," he continued, that it's *Adonai* Himself who accepts those who will do the will of *Adonai* or disowns people who do not. Not Yeshua!"[54] Putting my

---

[53] See Mark 3:32-35.

[54] Y'hudah is Yeshua's brother who wrote the Book of Jude in the New Testament, saying such as: *"I want to remind you, though you once knew this, that the Lord, having saved the people out of the land of Egypt, afterward destroyed those who did not believe"* (:5).

arms around *Ima* and my sister, I walked them toward home, the others following.

I seemed to have taken the role of eldest brother since Yeshua was no longer in that position. But I had no idea what to do or how to handle this situation. We were humiliated, all of us, and the concern for Him had turned now into more like rejection of Him. Yosef, sounding more hurt than anything else, managed to blurt out, "If He doesn't want us, then why should we want Him? As far as I'm concerned, He is no longer my brother," and he walked off, away from us. I couldn't tell if he seemed more like he was angry or was going to cry.

Ima, on the other hand, seemed even quieter than she had been since the synagogue episode. She seemed as if she was walking with her head held high and her shoulders thrown back, so her body language did not reflect any rejection. All she said was, "We will talk about this later. Let's not react until we have thought through what He said."

Not one to ever be disrespectful to *Ima*, this time I almost shouted at her as I responded to her. "Think it through? What's to think through, *Ima*? He flat out refused to see us. And what was that 'Who are my real family' nonsense?" *Ima* put up her hand and in the tone she used when she was *really* disciplining us when we were children she again said, "Do not react. Think about what He said and ask yourselves why He said it." My thoughts at that moment were that *Ima* was defending Him, providing an excuse to defuse the situation, though I knew she was deeply hurt.

As the days went on, we heard more and more stories, mostly by those who would pass through our village on their way to find Him or on their way back home after they did. People traveled for miles to hear what my brother had to say. We also heard of how so many people were healed, even hundreds of them. It would be hard not to believe what we were hearing as there were so many recounting the same things.

People would come by, willing to talk with anyone who would listen to them relate the miracles that were taking place, or what Yeshua had said, or the way He told a parable: "Not like the rabbis. His parables always caused you to look inside yourself, whereas the rabbis' parables were all about how righteous *they* were."[55] Someone added "He talks as if He knows *Yehova* in ways that the *Tzadukim* and the *P'rushim*[56] never knew Him." A number marveled at how Yeshua's face looked when He talked about *Yehova* – something I was familiar with. When I heard those words I suddenly had an awful feeling down deep inside that the people favoring Yeshua over the leaders was not going to bode well for Him, but it puzzled me as to what that could possibly mean.

---

[55] Parables were not exclusive to Yeshua. They were a common means of rabbinic teaching. As you read Yeshua's parables, keep in mind that His parables always had a surprise ending that made you see how well you met God's standard in them. The *Good Samaritan* story is a good example of who is really the righteous one whereas a rabbinic parable might have commended those who would uphold their added laws, such as to not touch the 'unclean' Samaritan, for instance.

[56] Sadducees and Pharisees.

One time I took a few days to go and find Him, which I did. What I saw was indeed extraordinary. He fed what must have been thousands of people with a scant few fish and a couple of bread rolls. At least that's what was being said. All I know is that everyone ate, but with all those people there was no way I could get through the crowd to even get near Him. Actually, I felt I had no right to go to Him. I was only a part of the crowd that day, not His brother. I watched Him with whom I had been so close with my entire life, until recently, like anyone watches as a spectator someone whose life you've never really encountered. And so, I came home again still bewildered as to all that was going on in His life.

To make matters worse, shortly thereafter it was as if we had lost our mother as we had always known her. She had finally shared with us the story of Yeshua's birth and the prophecies she had received at the temple when He was an infant, and how she and *Abba* had to escape to Egypt. We were dumbfounded as she unfolded the story to us. When had a family ever heard such an astounding story from their mother? If we had not known our *Ima* and what a valiant woman of *Yehova* she is, we might not have believed her. But she made the whole thing sound plausible as she revealed one incident after another. The capstone of the stories, of course, was that she was sure that Yeshua is the Messiah that Israel has been waiting for. How were we as her family to deal with *that* piece of information?

My brothers-in-law did not take this news of His birth very well which made it more difficult for my sisters. As close as my brothers and I were, it was for each of us to deal with this on our own. Soon after, with none of us children left at home to care for, on one of Yeshua's few homecoming visits, *Ima* decided that she was going with Him. And so, she began following Him wherever He went, careful to help take care of His needs and often those of His disciples, as she told us on one of her few visits back to us.

Only nothing He was doing met any of our ideas of what the Messiah would be like. Wouldn't Messiah do away with sin and the sinful? But, from what we were hearing, He seemed to call the sinners His friends. Wouldn't Messiah take His place in the temple, among the priests, with the *Tzadukim*? When neither He nor *Ima* came home for our family *Pesach Seder*,[57] it seemed to alienate us even more. We had never missed having our *Seder* dinners together, even in all our generations from Moshe[58] until these events with Yeshua. Now even our age-old tradition to be sure there was no leaven in our home, to which our shop was attached, for eight days was being disregarded as *Ima* was not there, though my sisters obeyed the commandment in their homes. Though we went through a *Seder* that year, no one really had a heart for it without *Ima* there.

How would all this end? What was to become of Yeshua... and of our *Ima*? My brothers had no more idea

---

[57] Yearly Passover meal and storytelling of the Exodus.

[58] See Exodus 12 re: Passover and Leaven. *Moshe*, pronounced *Mow-sheh*, is Moses in Hebrew with whom the first Passover took place. Jews have celebrated every year since.

what to do about or with Him than I did, and my sisters, well, they cried a lot and sometimes offered suggestions which, of course, would change nothing. It all seemed out of our hands. If He was the Messiah, why were we not rejoicing? Things certainly did not seem to be at all what we expected for the Messiah.

But then it happened. Not knowing we were His family, the news came with the travelers passing through our village. Hearing of His crucifixion was a paralyzing shock. I have no words for what it felt like to learn of it. There seemed no way to even begin to process such news. It was incomprehensible to think that our brother, our Yeshua, would be forced by the Romans to be so tortured, so humiliated, so shamed, and to die at their hands, even at His young age, and in such an unspeakable death as if He was a man cursed by God.[59] We were at a loss for words to speak, even to one another, of the horror of thinking of Him suffering like that. If only we had been able to get Him out of that house when we had gone to get Him to come home. If only... there were so many "if onlys." We were paralyzed with shock.

Then the shock turned to confusion and tormented my mind. Why would a Man who had created so much love for Himself so that people came from miles away to hear Him, or be touched by Him, and who were healed

---

[59] Deuteronomy 21:23 says, "...Cursed is *anyone who hangs on a tree ... his corpse shall not hang all night on the tree, but you shall surely bury him ... for he who is hanged is accursed of God; so that you do not defile your land .... bury him at sun setting."* What Yeshua experienced was being 'accursed by God' on our behalf.

just by His hands, be completely powerless when it came to those who wanted to do away with Him? Why? We knew He was controversial and somewhat challenging to the priesthood – the *T'zadakim* and to the *P'rushim*[60]. But what power did He have that caused the *P'rushim* to team up with the *T'zadakim* against Him when they had hated each other for years?

When we had just heard the news, we became paralyzed with how to process what we were hearing. So many questions arose. Why did He evoke such animosity among the leaders toward Him to the point that they wanted Him dead? The whole thing was beyond terrifying. It wasn't the *am haaretz,* the people of the land, whose children He had brought back to life, or those who had been healed of illness and paralyzes who would have wanted Him dead. Surely not. Nor would those who were fed fish and bread when they were hungry one long day. They certainly wouldn't have wanted Him crucified. I was there that day myself to see how much they loved and honored Him.

But those folks lived in the Galil[61] too far from *Yerushalayim*[62] to be able to testify on His behalf, not that it apparently would have mattered. From what we

---

[60] This was the only time the Sadducees (temple priests) and the Pharisees (teachers of the "law") were known to cooperate together, and it was against Yeshua.

[61] Galilee in Hebrew is Galil (Gah-LEEL).

[62] *Yerushalayim* is Jerusalem in Hebrew which was far from the *Galil* (Galilee) where many of those miracles took place. The voices shouting "Crucify Him" were not those who had loved Him, but those that were put up to it by those wanting Him dead.

heard, the so-called trial was a set-up, a hoax, and illegal by *Torah* standards. Nevertheless, He was convicted and crucified. It was beyond belief. Whatever it was that caused this to happen, it meant my brother suffered more than I would ever have wanted even for my worst enemy, and certainly not for Him. I cannot even describe the horror and the confusion this brought us.

I tried not to picture it or imagine how He dealt with the pain... and shame, and the suffocation.... When I allowed myself to try to picture what had taken place I could hardly breathe myself. I was unable to allow myself to picture further what He must have gone through. I had seen one person crucified and it was beyond horrible to look at. The profound hopelessness, the excruciating and unrelenting pain.... Even watching it was excruciating. And then I had an equally terrifying thought: Where was *Ima* when this was happening? *Where was Ima?!*

I wanted to go and find her, but we only heard of it a day or so after it happened, and we had no idea where to even look for her. What had become of Yeshua's *talmidim*?[63] Was she with them? Were they looking out for her? We immediately went to *Yerushalayim*[64] to try to find her but no one had any idea where she or His followers were. I was overwhelmed with the magnitude of all that had transpired. Still trying to make sense out of it all, I was now faced with how I was to find *Ima?*

---

[63] Disciples

[64] Jerusalem

What had become of her now that He was dead? We felt entirely helpless to rescue her, if, that is, she even wanted to be rescued. We just didn't know. We had heard something about Yeshua, even on the cross, giving care for her to one of His men. Some of His last words were apparently for her well-being. But what did that mean for us? Was she no longer our mother? My fears overwhelmed me and I felt paralyzed to change any of it.

My thoughts went back to Yeshua. This was my own brother who seems to have changed Israel – as if all seemed to be centered around Him. Whether for Him or against Him, adoring Him or hating Him, and it now appears, even though He was dead, still fearing Him as the leaders wanted to be sure He was dead. So, they made sure that His tomb had been secured by temple guards. He was still the talk of every man and woman in Jerusalem which quickly reached Nazareth by those who knew Him or knew of Him.

But no one in our village would even talk with us, knowing what had happened to Him. No one came to sit *shivah*[65] with us. They acted as if it hadn't happened. They seemed to share our shame and confusion but didn't know how to talk to us about it. Neither did we for that matter, even know how to talk about it with each other in the family.

---

[65] *Shivah* is a period of a week in which a Jewish family sits in mourning, while family and friends gather around them, often bringing food, to sit with them, often on the floor, while remembering (good things about) the deceased and saying prayers with the family. It is still a practice today.

I still couldn't make sense out of *why* it had all happened as it did. I knew the Scriptures well enough. Some of it fit for a Messiah. But not for my brother! How could it mean Yeshua - the one I shared most of my childhood with, the one I followed around as a young boy as my hero though He was only a few years older than I? There was never even the remotest idea or talk of Him being the Messiah. When *Ima* told us that miraculous story of His birth, I found a number of those events in the Scriptures. Astounding! But how could the Messiah's life, if indeed it was Yeshua, end the way it did? My thoughts turned over and over again and again. And then, just like a snap of the fingers, there He was, standing in front of me!

It was Yeshua, of that I was sure. He was the same height and had the same color hair. It was Him, yet there was ... how shall I say it? There was a sense of aliveness about Him that I'd never known on any other person, ever! There was certainly no trace of any of what He had just gone through, except for the mark where the nails had penetrated through His wrists. I stared at them for only a second – which made it all seem so real.

Then I noticed there was no sign of the weariness of life on His face, or of any age even though He wasn't much past thirty-three. He seemed... well, to say it again because it is so significant, more fully alive than I'd ever known anyone to be. Before I could process all this, I simply fell on my knees and bowed my face to the ground before Him. This was not something I would ever have done before, but this wasn't like before. *He* wasn't like He was before. I knew it was Yeshua but I had no concept in my mind to process what I was seeing in Him.

Then He said my name and I began to tremble, not even sure why. But then, I wasn't sure why of anything at this moment. He put His hand on my shoulder. When He touched me, I felt a strength coming into me. In a moment, I was able to sit up, though I was still on the floor before Him. Yes, this was my brother… No, He was no longer my brother, not as I had known Him all my life.

Here we were in our family home in the carpentry shop where we had been together all the years of our lives, but nothing was the same. All I can say now as I recall what took place is that He exuded life! Even the air around us seemed alive. I wanted to ask Him questions but before I could even formulate a thought, He began to speak to me.

I lost all sense of time then but later I realized how much He had conveyed to me in the time that He was with me. Somehow, He had made it all make sense, both our past together, the parents *Yehova* had given us, the ways our *Ima* on her own had taught us the things she did, and even what had been going on for the recent few years. If He had explained it all to us when He had to leave us, we would have attempted to alter what He was doing, as, in fact, we had tried.

Now I understood the words that He sent out to us when we tried to take Him home with us. We would have been in His way. We would have taken credit for being His family and all that would have been entirely contrary to His mission including the values He was trying to impart to Israel. As He gave me insight after insight, I understood it all now.

Then He showed me how *Yehova* would use me and all that we had learned together in those many hours we had talked and talked about the *Torah* and the prophets, and God's plan for Israel and how we were to live as His *Talmidim* and His representatives in the earth, even to the Romans. Now it all went together. The pieces of the puzzle not only made sense to me, but I was able to see how the great plan of *Yehova* for far more than just Israel was falling into place. While I did have some questions I was able to ask Him, all that He told me left me assured that I too had a place in God's plan and it would unfold for me as time went on. And then, just as He had come to me, in a moment, He was gone.

And so now, here I am, a leader of the believers in Yeshua, of the thousands who are now His followers, with the numbers growing daily. My expectation is that the world will be affected and that all Israel will be saved now that Messiah Yeshua has come. I am sure He will return one day soon enough to set up *Yehova's* Kingdom here in Jerusalem. In the meantime, there are folks elsewhere who are being persecuted for being His followers. And it is to them that I was writing.

I continued my story-telling to the two men who were still listening intently, though I had been doing more reminiscing than telling them what they didn't already know. I continued: Not everyone has become a believer in Yeshua. Even now, even after His resurrection, there are still rulers in Jerusalem who love their positions more than they love what was clearly of *Yehova*. And they are often, even in places far from Jerusalem, seeking after believers with the same evil aggressiveness with which they had crucified Yeshua.

Though He did not say so, Yeshua left me with the sense that I too would one day find myself in the position of giving my life for the truth of who He is. Only now, for the first time, death doesn't frighten me. It isn't an end, but a beginning of what is far beyond what this world offers us. I had witnessed in Yeshua that death had no permanency. He had faced it and in doing so He disarmed its power and threats and its condemnation and yes, it's permanency. And now, there is a never-ending Kingdom to access.

His resurrection means that death is not to be feared. It was not the end of His life but the beginning of true life – even in the aliveness that I saw in Him - as it will be for those of us who are His faithful followers. There is a life of perfection in *Yehova* outside of this sin-soaked life we live here on earth.

I see how so much of what had gone on in my life, even in *our* lives together, was designed and woven together by *Yehova* Himself to prepare me – even to prepare us, for His greater plan. Not just for my life, but for the lives of those even my own life will touch for Him. As I recalled what *Yehova* had tasked me with, to bring comfort and strength in Messiah to my fellow believers in Yeshua, my thoughts began to come together. Then suddenly I remembered that I had been telling all this to the two young men sitting in silent awe before me, who appeared to be mesmerized by my story.

With a renewed sense of purpose, anxious now to get this letter on its way, I dipped my quill pen into the inkwell before me as I began to write: *"My brethren, count it all joy when you fall into various trials, knowing that the testing of your faith produces patience. But let patience have its perfect work, that you may be perfect and complete, lacking nothing.*[66]

---

[66] James 1:1-4.

PART 2

Chapter 8

Why Yeshua Wept

Luke 10:39; John 7:36-50; 11:35

"There is no pain so great as the memory of joy in present grief"
-Aeschylus

This is Lonnie here, telling you this story. To be honest, I didn't want to share it or put it in this book – or any book. I treasured what the Lord showed me as deeply personal between us. But I felt that He wanted this shared so that others would know Him this intimately, this truthfully, so we would all know He was as human as we are. Many of us think of Yeshua as being just a bit too holy to be *really* fully human. Or to be somehow out of touch with our most human feelings.

In a time when, despite all my Bible knowledge, I really needed to know how much He could relate to my own humanity, I asked Him a number of questions. To be honest, if I wasn't surrounded by the circumstances I found myself in, I wouldn't have thought to even ask the questions I did. I believe the Lord lets us go through things in our lives at times in order to know Him in a way we would not even have a place for without the pain or anguish. Perhaps this is what Paul called *"the fellowship of His sufferings"* (Philippians 3:10).

In answer to my questions, surprised that He even began to answer as He did, the Lord began to show me what I would never have imagined on my own. What was revealed to me weaves together parts of the stories not woven together in the same way in the Gospels. But they went together in a believable whole that revealed a part of Yeshua I had never been aware of before. It all unfolded to me one scene at a time, as if I was watching it take place in my mind's eye, the way revelations sometimes come by the Holy Spirit. So, in the way that prophesies are to be confirmed or not, I leave it to you to decide whether this story bears the witness of the Holy Spirit.

It all began with seeing Miryam,[67] the sister of Lazarus and Martha, sitting at the feet of Yeshua.[68] Despite being a woman, she had the heart of a true disciple, wanting to learn as much as she could of *Yehova* from Him. His clear eyes seemed to her as if she could look back into the beginning of time, as if He knew things beyond what most people did. It wasn't what she saw, but what she sensed though she didn't understand why.

---

[67] Miryam, as pointed out earlier, is every biblical Mary's real name, including Yeshua's mother's.

[68] That she is said to have been "sitting at His feet" was a common term among rabbis and their disciples which any Jewish person would know. To sit at a rabbi's feet was to acknowledge that they were his disciple, which women never were – except for Miryam.

And she loved the sound of His voice uttering wisdom as no one else she'd ever known. Some have said she was worshiping Him, but worship was for *Yehova* alone and for no person. As godly as Yeshua might appear to her, He certainly wasn't understood to be God[69] as we know Him today and to have worshipped Him then would have been blasphemy. Worship belonged to *Yehova* only, never to a man. What shall we call what she was feeling for Him then? Respect, honor, even fascination. Perhaps gratefulness as we will see.

Seated on the floor before Him, surrounded by His disciples and others who were eager to listen to the things He had to say, sometimes He would look toward her to let her know He was addressing her too even though she was the only woman among the disciples. Miryam was still awed that He had set her free not only from the sinful ways in which she had been living, but He had made her clean again – pure as she had never been, even before she slid into sin. She hadn't intended things to go that way. It just happened, and she couldn't seem to get out of it.

If not for Yeshua the story of her life, and even how she would have died, could have gone much differently. Not only had He rescued her from a potential stoning by rocks being heaved at her till her bruised and broken body would have succumbed to death, but the words He spoke to her then, to *"go and sin no longer"*[70] had

---

[69] The Hebrew expectation was that Messiah would be a man just as Moses was a man. The few Old Testament Scriptures indicating Yeshua was God incarnate were only understood after His resurrection.

[70] John 8:11

transformed her. He spoke the words and it was as if they had power for her to just walk away from her life of sin. Just like that.

Whenever she heard Him speak since then, she could no longer even imagine doing what she had in the past. She wasn't the only one who was grateful for His rescue of her. Her brother and sister were no longer ashamed of her, and they too were grateful to Him as well for her return to them. And to *Yehova*.

But one thing was still a problem, at least when Yeshua was there, which was fairly often as their home was where He found rest and shelter from the growing crowds and their demands upon Him. Even there, when people found out He was in the area, crowds often gathered. He and Lazarus had become fast friends and often talked into the night about the things of *Yehova*. Miryam often made sure she was close enough to listen.

The problem was really that Miryam was of little help in doing the cooking or serving their guests whenever Yeshua was there. And Martha was increasingly resenting it. After all, Miryam had disappeared enough before Yeshua entered their lives, leaving Martha with the responsibility of running the house. And now that Miryam had changed her ways, she still wasn't being of very much help, at least when Yeshua was there.

But He had come to Miryam's rescue there too, speaking to Martha with the affectionate tone He always used for her, calling her, *"Martha, Martha."* Then He said to her in His gentle way, *"You are worried and troubled about many things. But one thing is needed, and,"* and nodding for a moment toward Miryam He added, *"Miryam has chosen that good part."* Martha would have been wounded by what He said to her but for the fondness for her in his voice. And then He added further, *"…which will not be taken away from her."*[71]

Was He protecting Miryam's *Yehova*-longing heart, not allowing it to be robbed by the mundane duties of providing food for Him and His men when an easily prepared meal could suffice without the elaborate preparations Martha was distracted with? From that moment on, Martha simplified the meals and no longer chided Miryam for not helping her with them, though Miryam was careful to help when Yeshua wasn't there. Peace restored!

With the tension of wishing she didn't have to help Martha now gone, listening to the timbre of His voice was like a melody to her heart, and the things He said fascinated her and made her feel as if it had been *Yehova* Himself Who had set her free. Yeshua's own love for Him poured out through His words. How she loved to hear all Yeshua spoke about Him as *Abba*. More and more she began to think of *Yehova* as Her own *Abba.* It was so easy to do so the way Yeshua spoke of Him, making it sound as if it was *Yehova's* own desire for everyone to know His love as Yeshua did. Whatever He said, Yeshua's words went deep into her heart and into her thoughts.

Very often Yeshua and His men would stay at their home after the other guests left and sleep there until

---

[71] Luke 10:41, 42

morning when they would be off again. Occasionally, after the disciples settled down for the night on their mats on the roof, she would find Yeshua standing in the moonlit garden looking out toward Jerusalem. At first, she just watched Him from afar, but in time, she wandered out to where He was and asked Him another question or two. His answers thrilled her and with each answer, there seemed to be more that she wanted to ask. At times, He seemed to speak as if He had been there when he told of *Yehova* speaking to Abraham, or Moshe or the prophets.

The more they talked, the more she began to feel closer to Him than she had ever felt toward any man before. This was different. *He* was different! He was holy, and honest, never deceitful or selfish, and never once did she ever sense anything like the way other men in the past would look at her. This was an entirely new and different way of relating to a man – one that was entirely pure. The more she was with Him, the more she sensed that He too felt a special bonding in their friendship, though she couldn't really identify any way that He was toward her than anyone else. Still, there was a comfortable easiness she felt between them she didn't even feel with Lazarus. Or, she wondered, was this the way He made all people feel?

She could not help but wonder what it would be like to be loved by such a man, to be His wife, to bear His children. Was that even possible? Would He want her after the past she'd had? There was no way to talk to Him about her feelings, and He never gave her any sense whatsoever that He entertained such thoughts, even if she thought she sensed a deepening in the things they shared of *Yehova* and of life.

And so, as I (Lonnie) 'watched' what I was perceiving in my spirit, I saw that it was Miryam whom Yeshua had saved from a stoning by the men who brought her to Him. I saw that she appreciated and loved Him for that and she came to love and respect Him even more for the Man He was, the Man who not only brought her out of the depths of sin but had now lifted her spirit and her thoughts high into understanding the ways of *Yehova* among men and angels. Who else could do that?

The next scene I saw was that of Lazarus who had died and was now in a grave for four days when Yeshua and His disciples finally arrived. It was, of course, after the fact. There was no healing him now. Not to Martha and Miryam or any of their neighbors who were mourning with them. The devastation was awful; his sisters' grief was almost unbearable. They had loved Lazarus deeply and now he was gone. Who would carry on the family name? The sisters had sent for Yeshua, of course, but He hadn't come until it was too late. Upon arriving at the area, four days later, Yeshua sent one of His disciples to their house with a message letting them know He was there.

Martha came immediately. We know the story. She came and said to Yeshua, "*If you had been here my brother would not have died.*"[72] She knows who He is; that is, she knows He is the only One who could have

---

[72] See John 11 for the whole story of Lazarus' death.

healed Lazarus. Yeshua speaks with her, informing her that He *is* the Resurrection and the Life, but to be fair, how could she possibly really understand that? Every Hebrew person, including Martha, knew there would be a final resurrection at the end of the age, so missing the deeper meaning of what He said, His words did not assuage her grief.

Then Yeshua asked for Miryam who evidently had not yet been made aware of His arrival. Martha went back to the house to tell her, *"The Master is here and He wants to see you."* With a leap to her feet from where she was sitting *shiva*[73] on the floor, she ran to where Yeshua is waiting for her. Now here is where we really begin to see behind the scenes.

Miryam comes to Him and says the same words her sister did, thoughts that no doubt the sisters had expressed to each other numerous times: *"If you had been here, Lazarus would not have died."* The J.B. Phillips bible then says, *"And looking into His eyes, she fell at His feet."* Evidently, she is completely undone, in unbearable grief. If only He had been there. It is here the Bible tells us that *"Yeshua wept."*[74] The word for wept here means to shed silent tears. Miryam is at His feet and He is moved to the point of tears streaming down his cheeks.

---

[73] *Shiva*, as mentioned before, is a time of mourning for up to a week when Jewish people would often sit on the floor or a low bench while friends and family came around them, bringing food, and just being with the bereaved and joining in a time of praying the *kaddish*, a prayer said that gives glory to *Adonai* even though the person has died.

[74] John 11:35.

What exchanged between them in that one swift moment when she looked into His eyes that caused Him to respond as deeply as He did? Was it her love for Him and trust in Him, despite Lazarus' death, that evoked His response? Surely there was no accusation, only sorrow. Whatever He felt at that moment when confronted with Miryam's tears and her overwhelming grief, it evoked something in Him that caused Him to shed His own tears. As I watched this picture unfold in my mind's eye, she is again at His feet. Not as a disciple this time but in great angst, as she is weeping audibly in her grief over the loss of her brother.

At this I became aware of what He may have been feeling. He knows He will be crucified within a very short time. He sees the devastating grief she is experiencing now at Lazarus' death, though He already knows He will raise Lazarus from the dead and give him back to her and Martha. But He will not be given back to her after He dies. He knows of her love for Him and what it is that they share. He knows full well. And He knows what she will feel when she finds out that He has died the excruciating death He is destined for? If Lazarus' death is unbearable for her now, what will His horrific death do to her?

Perhaps He becomes more acutely aware at that moment than He may have been aware before, of the shock and the excruciating agony, she will go through when she learns of His death? What will it do to her to learn of the torture He will experience and of the suffering and the shame of the crucifixion? It is then that He weeps. Not for Himself, but for her. Not for His own suffering, but for hers.

Yes, He will be raised from death and live again, but not for three long agonizing days, or however long it will be till she is told He is alive. Even so, no longer will He be her friend to walk with, to talk with, and to share things of *Yehova* with as they have. He knows that no matter how glorious the outcome of His resurrection will be, the friendship they have had will only be memories for her and that she will continue to miss Him for the rest of her life. If Yeshua felt any grief about His own death on a human level, of having to leave the people He loves, it may be right here, for what others will go through.

I sensed that His own feelings caused Him to want to protect her. It is not because He loved Lazarus so much that He wept, as the people thought, or because He saw how the people were grieving over Lazarus, but because He loved her the only way He could. The distinct sense that I had at that moment as this was unfolding before me was that what He wished He could do was pick her up in His strong carpenter arms and carry her away from all that present and soon-to-come anguish and sorrow.

But He could not. He could not even hold her to comfort her as He longed to, for that would have entered a place of intimacy between them that would later make her pain worse when He was no longer there. No more would He be the friend to her that He had been, no longer sharing the things of *Yehova* with her as no one else would ever be able to.

He would no longer come and share meals and evenings of song and laughter and Bible stories with her and her family. I sensed that at that point, Yeshua felt all the loss that His leaving would mean. And again, I felt that His hurting was not for Himself - never for Himself - but for her. And perhaps for the others who loved Him who would not know of His resurrection for several very long excruciated and confusing days.

And then the scene changed to another situation altogether. It took place in the home of *Shimon*[75] who is identified as a leper, though obviously, he is no longer a leper. He is likely giving a dinner in Yeshua's honor for having healed him. He appears to live in the same village as Martha, Miryam, and Lazarus who is now healthy. A number of people are there for a celebration. Whatever the occasion, this is the scene in which a woman who is identified as a sinner in one Gospel account is also referred to by John as "...*that Mary (Miryam) who anointed the Lord with fragrant oil and wiped His feet with her hair, whose brother Lazarus was sick.*"[76]

I did not, however, make the connection that this was Miryam when I first saw this taking place. I only saw that at some point during this gathering a woman begins to weep and wash Yeshua's feet with her tears, wiping them with her hair. She is also anointing them with very expensive oil, likely an oil kept by the family for burial purposes as was the custom. It only then came to me as I watch this taking place, that this woman is Miryam. What follows reveals the dark heart of at least one of those watching in what is likely the recounting of the

---

[75] Simon in English, pronounced Shee-mown.
[76] John 11:2,3. Also see Mark 14:8.

purest expression of any person's love for Yeshua in the entire Bible.

As this act appears to be a rather sensuous thing to do, which no doubt caught everyone's attention, it evidently was not seen for what it truly was to anyone but Yeshua. Despite that her life had entirely turned around to righteousness, what is taking place triggers in the mind of at least one man some old memories of what kind of woman she was before Yeshua came into her life. Evidently, Yeshua's forgiveness and her new life were oblivious to this man.

She, however, is only aware of Yeshua and her ministry to Him, and her overwhelming grief in anticipation of His death. He being a Man of no unholy inclinations, relates to what she is doing as an expression of utmost purity. He makes a significant statement: "*She has done what she could. She has come beforehand to anoint My body for burial.*"

What has He told her? She evidently understands that within days He will die and be buried. He did tell His men more than once what was ahead. How is it that she is the only one in the entire gospel story who seems to act as if she grasps the reality of it? He had wept in anticipate of her suffering-to-come, now she is weeping over His, both expressions of pure and unselfish love for one another. God's kind of love.

How much had He told her of what was going to take place? That He would die? Yes, evidently. But how much more? He would want to spare her, of course, so perhaps not about the beatings and the torturing. Could He have told her *why* He had to die? Would that be far too much for her to comprehend? Perhaps. Even so, He had evidently tried to prepare her with whatever words that now had her weeping as she was anointing Him for His burial. It seems that whatever the extent of her knowledge of the end of His life, she knows He's going to die. She knows that!

Nothing will change what is ahead and she can do nothing to stop it. Yet, Yeshua makes it clear that what she was doing was the one thing she could intentionally do for Him. She anointed this Man whom she loved and honored with all her heart for His death.

Then I heard Judas, the man with the attitude, who is also the disciple who carried their money, speak against her with the pretense that the *shekels*[77] the oil she had just poured upon Him would be worth could be better used to feed the poor. We all know Judas by now, so we know his intentions were dishonorable, but what I came to know next gave me an entirely different perspective on what took place after that.

As Judas speaks against her, I "heard" Yeshua's words, *"Leave her alone"* as if He had *roared* them at Judas. That's the word that came to my mind at the moment Yeshua spoke, that He actually *roared* at Judas, infuriated with him, as He punctuated each word, enunciating, *"LEAVE…HER…ALONE!!!"*

That's when Yeshua said, *"I assure you that wherever the Gospel is preached throughout the whole world, this deed of hers will also be recounted, as her memorial to*

---

[77] Money

me."[78] At that moment I understood that what He had just said was to give her the highest honor that He ever gave to anyone. What He could not give to her in this life, He gave to her in a place of honor with and near Him in the Gospels, even in that most significant moment in His life. He made her a woman of great valor and respect, for all who would know His story for all times would also know of her.

It came to me that this profound story is one of a woman who's broken and sinful life was so turned around by His forgiveness and love that she is the quintessential picture of all sinful lives made precious in His sight.

But the revelation didn't end there. What came next stunned me differently than all the rest. Yeshua was speaking of His honor of her, as we have just seen. Then the verse immediately following this episode appears to provide the answer to a "Why?" about which believers have speculated over for centuries. Read it and see what I mean. Here's what is recorded again and what follows:

"Assuredly, I say to you, wherever this gospel is preached in the whole world, what this woman has done will also be told as a memorial to her." Then one of the twelve, called Judas Iscariot, went to the chief priests and said, "What are you willing to give me if I deliver Him to you?" And they counted out to him thirty pieces of silver. (Matthew 26:13-15).

---

[78] Mark 14:9-11

Do you see it? Do you see that the "Then" connects the two events? When Yeshua rebuked Judas and roared at Him to leave her alone, Judas was humiliated and so he reacted with the evil intention to vindicate himself. Judas felt that Yeshua had rebuked Him publicly, giving respect to her, a woman that in Judas' mind was certainly unworthy of being given respect, and certainly not above himself, and this brought a rage of indignation to Judas. I sensed that I was being shown that Judas' attitude was as if he said to himself, "How dare He ridicule me like that in front of everyone and give honor to *that* woman!"

If we ever wondered what motivated Judas to turn against Yeshua, this is likely to be the reason right here. He was offended, humiliated, and shamed in front of everyone there. The core of the issue was Judas' pride. Another verse says, "*After this*" and then goes on to say, "*one of the twelve, Judas Iscariot by name, approached the chief priests. "What will you give me," he said to them, "if I hand him over to you?" They settled with him for thirty silver coins, and from then on he looked for a convenient opportunity to betray Yeshua.*"[79]

The distinct sense that I had was that Judas was so indignant at what had taken place that he went to the priests having already turned against Yeshua in his heart and was seeking to get back at Yeshua for humiliating him, all for thirty pieces of silver. The rest of his story is a tragedy.

---

[79] Matthew 26:14-16

But we are not left with Judas's story. What we come away with is the deep sense of the protective love Yeshua had for Miryam and the purity of her love for Him. Perhaps she was the only person with whom He could share *Yehova* in the ways that they did. Not in a teaching, but a sharing. After all, she had experienced the forgiveness and new life at a profound life-altering level. Her understanding of the grace of *Abba* and His caring for those with broken lives had permeated her entire life and her very being. Yeshua's words had to have resonated within her not only as *His* truth, but also now as *her* own identity and truth.

How she later processed the profound reality that *Yehova* had come to earth as a Man and He was the Man she loved, we cannot begin to comprehend, though it is certainly worthy of pondering, isn't it?

Epilogue

Sometime after I wrote this last chapter the Lord had me share it at a *Women's Aglow* meeting where I was scheduled to speak. I hadn't originally planned for this to be my message, but I felt the Lord was asking me to share it. A deep and luscious sense of the Spirit's presence was in the meeting as we worshipped and as I shared this story. A kind of a hush of respect for the dignity and revelation the story carries seemed to hover over us. After I shared the story we went back into worship so each of us could process with the Lord the meaning it had for us.

There was a deep sobbing from one woman off in a corner on her knees. Later she told me that she saw herself as the woman He loved who also loved Him so unashamedly. And then, she heard in her spirit the Lord *roar* at the devil, saying, "Leave her alone!" It was a kind of deliverance for her, setting her apart as His! The reason for her sobbing was the release she felt now knowing of His protective love for her.

Perhaps someone reading these stories needs to know Yeshua loves you like He loved her, or the others in these stories. Each story represents someone who may have been sinful, or unbelieving, or broken in some way. Or perhaps too hurt or angry to trust. And yet, when we take the risk to let Him in, or we welcome Him easily into our lives, perhaps as we come to know Him in ways that we've not known Him before, we find out how deeply He cares and how He meets us right where we are, at any time and without judgment, and always with His welcoming arms.

I believe the biblical stories, including ones we elaborate on like these, have been given to us for layers of reasons. The sweetest one is for each of us to find the Lord personally, to come to know Him more and more in the various ways that He can be known, including through the biblical stories. Finding Him in ways we didn't know Him before is one of life's greatest never-ending delights!

May I suggest that you consider writing your own *Jesus: Life Changer!* stories of where He has been in your life and situations. It doesn't matter if you write well. Just write for yourself and the Lord. That's how I started writing. Doing so might help make you more aware of what He's doing in your life.

You, my friend, are one of His miracles. These were ordinary people in these stories, just like you and me. What made their lives so meaningful? Jesus – Life Changer! He's still doing the same thing today.

If perhaps you are stirred to wanting to know Yeshua more than you do, especially if knowing Him personally is a new experience for you, would you pray this simple prayer with me to come close to Him, or pray with your own words:

Lord, I ask you to forgive me for living so independently of You. And please forgive me for any ways I have been that I now know were not pleasing to You. Thank you, Jesus, for dying on the cross to pay for my own sins so that I can now have a relationship with Father God and with You. I release all my failures to you now and thank you for making me a new "born again" person. Please come into my life and be my Lord. I thank you for giving me Your Holy Spirit to teach me all I need to know to be filled with Your love and to live in the forgiveness You have given to me and to extend it to others so I hold nothing against anyone else. I don't really understand all this yet, Lord, but thank you for showing me how to walk in the power of the Holy Spirit so I can live an overcoming life in You. In Yeshua's name. Amen.

If you have prayed that prayer or used your own words to pray and would like to tell me, I would be happy to hear from you and will respond to you. You can email me at WritingdowntheLane@gmail.com. Please put "Prayed the Prayer" in the subject line so I don't miss your email. I look forward to hearing from you.

May His great love be your firm foundation.

Lonnie

About the Author

LONNIE LANE

Lonnie Lane as a Jewish believer in Messiah Yeshua, writes from Jesus' own Jewish background. As the author of several books and over two-hundred articles, she considers that she has inherited the gift of being a scribe for the Lord from her father's "Levite" genes.

Lonnie is an ordained pastor, a Bible teacher and speaker in churches, conferences and home fellowships with a heart to help nurture an Acts 3:21 Restoration to prepare for the Lord's return. She was a past Producer of Sid Roth's *Its Supernatural* TV shows and served as the "Hebrew Roots Pastor" at The River Church, Jacksonville, Florida, for a number of years.

Among her other writings Lonnie is the author of *Because They Never Asked: A Jewish Family's Search for God*, and *Heaven is Beyond Your Wildest Expectations*, co-authored with Sid Roth. She also worked with Alyosha Ryabinov as editor of his book, *Thinking Hebraically*. Under a pen name she collected and edited a book of stories of Muslims who have come to faith in Jesus. She is also the author of *Meeting Jesus-Knowing God*, a discipleship course, and *The Majesty of Humility*, a book of her poetry.

Her latest book, *Being One--Tasting Joy: Preparation for Messiah's Return* should be released early in 2019.

To contact Lonnie: Lonnielane316@gmail.com.

CPSIA information can be obtained
at www.ICGtesting.com
Printed in the USA
LVHW032202011218
598945LV00002B/82/P